Test Your
BIBLE
Knowledge

Test Your
BIBLE
Knowledge

Carl S. Shoup

VALUEBOOKS
An Imprint of Barbour Publishing, Inc.

© 1971 by Fleming H. Revell Company

Print ISBN 978-1-61626-967-8

eBook Editions:
Adobe Digital Edition (.epub) 978-1-62029-452-9
Kindle and MobiPocket Edition (.prc) 978-1-62029-451-2

Scripture quotations in this volume are from the King James Version of the Bible.

Published by Value Books, an imprint of Barbour Publishing, Inc., P.O. Box 719, Uhrichsville, Ohio 44683, www.barbourbooks.com

Our mission is to publish and distribute inspirational products offering exceptional value and biblical encouragement to the masses.

Member of the
Evangelical Christian
Publishers Association

Printed in the United States of America.

Preface

If you have some knowledge of the Bible, or would like to learn something about it, this book invites you to a game of multiple choice. A statement based on the Scriptures is begun and is completed by four different endings. Only one of the endings is correct. Which one?

A Biblical scholar will probably have no difficulty in selecting the right ending for virtually every one of the 1,437 statements presented here. Those who are fairly well acquainted with the Bible will no doubt pick the correct ending in the majority of cases. Others presumably will have more difficulty. But even one who is not at all acquainted with the Scriptures will find in these statements so much that is familiar he may well score better than he might expect.

Bible tests have hitherto consisted of a series of questions, sometimes to be answered by yes or no, sometimes requiring a rather detailed reply. But questions piled one upon another tend to become wearisome. Also, there is not much fun in searching one's memory repeatedly. To test our powers of recognition, on the other hand, rather than our powers of recall, can become an enjoyable pastime in which the reader matches wits with the author. Therefore, the three incorrect endings have usually been worded with an eye to making them seem as plausible as possible. Sometimes these false endings are merely passages lifted from nearby Scripture verses. More often they are pure fabrication.

This test had its origin in the writer's realization that he had been harboring a vast number of misconceptions and garbled memories of a book he thought he had absorbed so freely in his youth. Some of these misconceptions suggested incorrect yet plausible endings to statements based on the Scriptures. Error is not always a promising base from which to evoke truth, but discovery of error proved in this instance to have a certain stimulative value.

All of the statements and the correct endings, as well as some of the incorrect endings, are either based on or quoted directly from the *King James Version of the Bible*. When reference to a Bible dictionary was needed, *A Dictionary of the Bible* by John D. Davis was used.

This multiple-choice test could not have been produced without the editorial and research assistance provided by Mrs. Carolyn S. Scott. She has contributed immeasurably to the final product.

CARL S. SHOUP

Test Your
Bible
Knowledge

Genesis

✔ ✔ ✔ ✔ ✔ ✔ ✔ ✔

1. **On the first day, God**   [Genesis 1:3–5]
   a said, "Let there be light"
   b created the dry land called Earth
   c made the two great lights, to rule the day and the night
   d created the firmament

2. **The firmament was**   [Genesis 1:6–8]
   a Earth
   b the space between Heaven and Earth
   c Heaven
   d the two great lights

3. **On the third day, God**   [Genesis 1:11–13]
   a created the great whales
   b said, "Let the earth bring forth grass"
   c created cattle and creeping things and beasts of the earth
   d created man

4. **On the sixth day, God**   [Genesis 1:26–27, 31]
   a said, "Let fowl fly above the earth"
   b created herbs and fruit trees
   c created man
   d rested

5. **God formed man of**   [Genesis 2:7]
   a clay
   b mud
   c dust
   d detritus

6. **The tree, the fruit of which man was forbidden to eat, was the tree of**   [Genesis 2:9, 17]
   a knowledge of good and evil
   b knowledge of evil
   c evil
   d life

7. **Of the four rivers that branched from the river of Eden, one was the**   [Genesis 2:10–14]
   a Euphrates
   b Abanah
   c Jordan
   d Halys

8. **God made woman**   [Genesis 2:18–22]
   a   to aid man in his struggle against the serpent
   b   because no help meet for man was found among the beasts of the field and the fowl of the air
   c   because man had been created with too many ribs
   d   to endow mankind with the symmetry of the heavenly bodies

9. **God made woman by taking from Adam**
                                          [Genesis 2:21–22]
   a   one rib
   b   two ribs
   c   three ribs
   d   four ribs

10. **In the specific language of Genesis, a man and his wife become one flesh, as the father and mother are left by**
                                          [Genesis 2:24]
   a   the man, who cleaves to his wife
   b   the woman, who cleaves to her husband
   c   both the man and woman, who cleave to each other
   d   neither, who nevertheless cleave to each other

11. **Adam and the woman became aware that they were naked**
                                          [Genesis 3:6–8]
   a   after talking with the serpent, but before eating the forbidden fruit
   b   after talking with the Lord God
   c   just before talking with the serpent
   d   after eating the forbidden fruit, but before talking with the Lord God

12. **When the Lord God made inquiry, the** [Genesis 3:12–13]
   a   man blamed the woman
   b   woman blamed the man
   c   man blamed the serpent
   d   serpent claimed he had said not a word

13. **"For dust thou art, and unto dust shalt thou return," said the Lord God to**   [Genesis 3:17, 19]
   a   Adam
   b   the woman
   c   Adam and the woman
   d   the serpent

14. **Adam called his wife Eve because**   [Genesis 3:20]
   a   she came after God had caused a deep sleep to fall upon Adam
   b   she was the mother of all living
   c   it was evening, when the Lord God questioned them
   d   the word "eve" signifies in Hebrew, "woman"

15. **When Adam and Eve were driven out of the Garden of Eden, they were wearing**   [Genesis 3:21]
   a   coats of skins

    b   aprons of fig leaves
    c   sandals of snake skin
    d   nothing

16. **Adam and Eve were expelled from the Garden of Eden
     to prevent them from**   [Genesis 3:22–23]
    a   repeating their previous offense
    b   eating of the tree of life
    c   remaining under the influence of the serpent
    d   believing they could disregard the Lord's edicts with
        impunity

17. **Cain quarrelled with Abel because**   [Genesis 4:3–5]
    a   Abel had been made a keeper of sheep, but Cain only
        a tiller of the ground
    b   Abel claimed a half-share in the property set aside for
        the sons
    c   Abel taunted Cain on his vicious habits
    d   the Lord accepted Abel's offering, but not Cain's

18. **"Am I my brother's keeper?" asked**   [Genesis 4:9]
    a   Abel of Adam
    b   Abel of the Lord
    c   Cain of Adam
    d   Cain of the Lord

19. **The Lord set a mark upon Cain to**   [Genesis 4:14–15]
    a   protect him against murder
    b   warn others against him
    c   identify him as a tiller of the soil
    d   disfigure him

20. **The land of Nod was**   [Genesis 4:16]
    a   where Cain had raised the fruit of the ground he
        offered to the Lord
    b   where Abel was buried
    c   where Cain went, after he killed Abel
    d   the term Adam used, to refer to Eden

21. **Evidently, Abel had**   [Genesis 4:8, 17–26]
    a   no descendants
    b   one descendant
    c   two descendants
    d   three descendants

22. **Adam had**   [Genesis 5:4; 4:1–2, 25]
    a   two sons
    b   three sons
    c   three sons and one daughter
    d   more than four children

23. **Methuselah lived**   [Genesis 5:5, 27]
    a   39 years longer than Adam
    b   515 years longer than Adam
    c   907 years longer than Adam
    d   203 years less than Adam

24. **After men began to multiply, the Lord decided that the life span of man was to be**   [Genesis 6:1–3]
    a   70 years
    b   90 years
    c   120 years
    d   900 years

25. **As to the creatures that were taken on board the ark,**
    [Genesis 6:7, 13, 17, 19–20; 7:2–4, 8–9, 14–16, 21–23; 8:1, 17–21; 9:10; 1:21; cf. 9:2]
    a   fish were specifically included
    b   fish were specifically excluded
    c   fish were not specifically mentioned, although sea-life had been created
    d   fish were not specifically mentioned, sea-life apparently not having yet been created

26. **The only human beings allowed in the ark were**
    [Genesis 6:18]
    a   Noah, his wife, his sons, and his sons' wives
    b   Noah, his sons, and his sons' wives
    c   Noah, his wife, his sons and daughters, and their spouses
    d   Noah and his wife

27. **The Lord never instructed Noah, with respect to the creatures he took on board the ark, to take more than**
    [Genesis 7:2–3]
    a   one pair of each
    b   two pairs of each
    c   one pair of some, two pairs of others
    d   one pair of some, eight pairs of others

28. **It rained for**   [Genesis 7:4, 12]
    a   150 days and nights
    b   40 days and nights
    c   40 days
    d   40 nights

29. **After the ark had grounded on Mt. Ararat, Noah and his passengers had to wait inside for the earth to become dry so that they could leave the ark,**   [Genesis 8:4, 14–18]
    a   more than half a year
    b   less than half a year but more than two months
    c   forty days
    d   one week

30. **The bird that by her actions finally let Noah know that all was well was the**   [Genesis 8:6–12]
    a   raven
    b   dove
    c   swallow
    d   gull

31. **The Lord's promise to Himself never to smite again every thing living was made** [Genesis 8:21–22]
    a   unconditionally
    b   dependent on man's use of his knowledge
    c   valid until Armageddon
    d   with a few exceptions

32. **The rainbow was devised as** [Genesis 9:12–17]
    a   a symbol of the Lord's promise never to flood the earth again
    b   an indication to Noah that the rain was about to cease
    c   a help to the dove to find its way back to the ark
    d   a signal of the birth of Shem, Ham, and Japheth

33. **The three men from whom the whole earth was overspread after the flood were** [Genesis 9:18–19]
    a   Ham, Japheth, and Shem
    b   Ham, Japheth, and Seth
    c   Enoch, Japheth, and Shem
    d   Ham, Lamech, and Shem

34. **Noah put a curse on his grandson Canaan because**
    [Genesis 9:20–27]
    a   Canaan seized land belonging to his brother Egypt
    b   Canaan slew Tubal
    c   Canaan's father saw the nakedness of his father
    d   Ham stole the garment his brothers had put on Noah

35. **Nimrod was** [Genesis 10:9–10]
    a   a mighty fisherman
    b   one whose kingdom included Babel
    c   a grandson of Noah's
    d   a graven image

36. **The city of Babel was so named because** [Genesis 11:1–9]
    a   it was so gigantic a project, men from foreign lands with strange tongues were brought in to work on it
    b   it was alarming evidence of what a common-language mankind could do; hence, the Lord scattered the workers by creating differences in language
    c   its tower was used as a platform from which many prophets harangued the multitude
    d   the architect's name was Babel

37. **Abram was of the** [Genesis 11:10–26]
    a   third generation after Noah
    b   tenth generation after Noah
    c   fifty-second generation after Noah
    d   two hundred forty-first generation after Noah

38. **Abram was Lot's** [Genesis 11:27]
    a   grandfather
    b   uncle
    c   godfather
    d   great-uncle

39. **Entering Egypt to escape the famine, Abram persuaded his wife Sarai to pass as his sister, in order to**
[Genesis 12:10–16]
   a   obtain certain preferences at Pharaoh's court granted only to single men
   b   get two single rations of food during the famine instead of one and one-half
   c   avoid ridicule as the husband of a barren wife
   d   escape death if the Egyptians seized Sarai

40. **Abram and Lot could not dwell together on the parcel of land between Bethel and Hai because**   [Genesis 13:1–6]
   a   they were both too rich
   b   they were both too poor
   c   Abram was so much richer than Lot
   d   Lot was so much richer than Abram

41. **When the Lord gave to Abram and to his seed for ever all the land that he could see in the land of Canaan, from the spot where he was, He promised Abram that his descendants would be as the**   [Genesis 13:14–16]
   a   leaves of the trees
   b   pebbles on the beach
   c   dust of the earth
   d   locusts in Egypt

42. **Lot's choice of Sodom as a place to live turned out to be a poor one; he**   [Genesis 14:8–12; 13:12]
   a   was captured by neighboring kings who raided Sodom and Gomorrah
   b   fell into a tar pit near Sodom
   c   was turned into a pillar of salt
   d   died in a famine

43. **Ishmael was the**   [Genesis 16:3–4, 11; 25:12]
   a   son of Hagar
   b   brother of Hagar
   c   son of Isaac
   d   son of Abraham's brother

44. **Sarai was angry with Abram because Hagar, her maid,**
[Genesis 16:5]
   a   was seduced by Abram
   b   having conceived, despised Sarai
   c   was sent back to Egypt by Abram
   d   was promised, for her child, one-half of Abram's property

45. **Hagar was told by the angel to name her son Ishmael because the Lord**   [Genesis 16:11]
   a   was dissatisfied with her
   b   had heard her affliction
   c   destined him for the battlefield
   d   desired to reproach Sarai

46. **Ishmael and Isaac were**   [Genesis 16:15; 21:3]
    a   cousins
    b   half brothers
    c   father and son
    d   brothers

47. **Abraham and Sarah were**   [Genesis 17:5, 15]
    a   the son and daughter of Abram and Sarai
    b   Abram and Sarai, before a change in their names
    c   strangers to Abram and Sarai
    d   Abram and Sarai, after God changed their names

48. **Circumcision was required by the Lord**   [Genesis 17:9–14]
    a   as an indication of His covenant with Abraham
    b   for reasons of health
    c   as a substitute for sacrifice of the firstborn
    d   to celebrate the birth of a son to Isaac

49. **At the Lord's announcement to Abraham that he would
    have a son by Sarah, Abraham fell on his face' and
    laughed for**   [Genesis 17:15–17]
    a   gratitude
    b   incredulity
    c   disappointment
    d   relief

50. **God promised Abraham that one of his sons would be
    the father of twelve princes; namely,**   [Genesis 17:20]
    a   Isaac
    b   Ishmael
    c   Mamre
    d   a son as yet unnamed

51. **Sarah's laughter at the announcement that she would
    have a son was followed by**   [Genesis 18:9–15]
    a   laughter from the Lord
    b   laughter from Abraham
    c   laughter from bystanders
    d   a dispute with the Lord over whether she had laughed

52. **Abraham, having persuaded the Lord to spare Sodom
    if fifty righteous persons could be found in it,**
                                        [Genesis 18:23–32]
    a   got permission from the Lord to warn Lot and his
        family to leave Sodom
    b   sent his son Isaac in to search for fifty righteous per-
        sons
    c   repented of his action, and persuaded the Lord to
        destroy Sodom if fifty wicked could be found
    d   argued on with the Lord until he got the number
        down to ten

53. **When all the men of Sodom surrounded Lot's house to
    get at the two angels (men) who were stopping there
    overnight, Lot**   [Genesis 19:1–8]

    a   offered his two virgin daughters to the crowd if they
         would leave his guests alone

    b   hid the two men in his granary and let the crowd into
         his house

    c   turned his house into a pillar of fire and barely
         escaped alive

    d   turned the two men over to the crowd

54. **As Lot and his family fled from Sodom,**   [Genesis 19:26]
    a   because Lot looked back, he was turned to a pillar
         of salt

    b   because Lot's wife looked back, she was turned to a
         pillar of salt

    c   because Lot looked back, his wife was turned to a
         pillar of salt

    d   because his wife looked back, Lot was turned to a
         pillar of salt

55. **Lot's daughters made him drunk with wine, so that**
                                      [Genesis 19:30–38]
    a   he would not try to pursue the avenging angels who
         had destroyed his city

    b   they would preserve offspring through their father, no
         other men being left to them

    c   they would gain his consent to seek husbands in
         strange lands

    d   they could steal back to the ruins of Sodom

56. **Moab was Lot's**   [Genesis 19:36–37]
    a   nephew and uncle
    b   father and uncle
    c   son and grandson
    d   brother and nephew

57. **Entering Gerar, Abraham persuaded his wife Sarah to**
pass as his sister, in order to   [Genesis 20:1–13]
    a   obtain certain preferences at King Abimelech's court
         granted only to single men

    b   get two single rations of food during the famine in-
         stead of one and one-half

    c   avoid ridicule as the husband of a barren wife

    d   escape death if the Gerarites seized Sarah

58. **Sarah was, in fact,**   [Genesis 20:12]
    a   a sister of Abraham's
    b   a half-sister of Abraham's
    c   a sister of Abraham's by adoption
    d   no sister at all to Abraham

59. **When Sarah urged Abraham to cast out Hagar and her**
son, God told Abraham that   [Genesis 21:9–12]
    a   He agreed with her
    b   He disagreed with her
    c   it was up to Abraham to decide
    d   only Hagar's son should go

60. **Hagar cast her child under a shrub and sat down a good way off** [Genesis 21:15–16]
   a to hide him from Sarah's servants
   b so that he might be found by Abraham's servants
   c because she could carry him no further
   d to spare herself the sight of his dying

61. **Beersheba was** [Genesis 21:25–31]
   a a dissolute queen from the region of the upper Nile
   b the well of the oath, where Abraham made a covenant with the local king
   c a desert region of the Negeb, south of Kadesh
   d Isaac's older daughter

62. **On their way to the place of sacrifice, Isaac said to his father, "Behold the fire and the wood; but where is the** [Genesis 22:3, 6–7]
   a water?"
   b rope?"
   c lamb?"
   d altar?"

63. **As Abraham was about to slay Isaac, he looked up, having heard an angel call from heaven, and saw** [Genesis 22:10–13]
   a the Lord
   b the angel
   c a ram
   d Ishmael

64. **"God will provide" refers to the fact that He provided Abraham with a** [Genesis 22:8, 13]
   a son
   b food
   c descendants
   d ram

65. **At the watering place, Abraham's servant selected Rebekah as the one he would ask to marry Isaac because** [Genesis 24:14–20]
   a she offered both him and his camels a drink
   b she knew enough to refrain from offering water to camels
   c she gave him a drink at his request, and offered water for the camels
   d she warned the servant that the water was not potable

66. **When Isaac was born to him, Abraham was "in his old age," at 100 years; Abraham died at the age of** [Genesis 21:2, 5; 25:7, 8]
   a 102
   b 133
   c 175
   d 361

67. **Ishmael lived longer than**
                    [Genesis 25:17; 23:1; 25:7; and see No. 23]
    a   Sarah
    b   Abraham
    c   Adam
    d   Methuselah

68. **When Jacob followed Esau out of his mother's womb he was gripping Esau's**   [Genesis 25:23–26]
    a   ankle
    b   heel
    c   wrist
    d   hair

69. **The reason Esau gave for selling his birthright to Jacob for bread and pottage was that he**   [Genesis 25:29–34]
    a   knew of the Lord's prophecy that he would serve Jacob
    b   disliked responsibility
    c   thought Jacob could not prove the bargain
    d   thought he was about to die

70. **When Isaac moved to Gerar he passed his wife Rebekah off as his sister because**   [Genesis 26:6–7]
    a   she was his sister
    b   he was afraid that otherwise the men would kill him, to get her
    c   "sister" was a generic term in Geraric for female companions generally
    d   she would have a wider social life

71. **The skins of kids were put upon Jacob's hands to**
                    [Genesis 27:11–23]
    a   protect him while hunting
    b   make Isaac think that Jacob was Esau
    c   cure him of erysipelas
    d   make Esau think that Jacob was Isaac

72. **When Jacob awoke after dreaming of a ladder to heaven, he promised to give the Lord a tenth of all that**
                    [Genesis 28:12, 22]
    a   the Lord gave to him
    b   his father gave to him
    c   he earned by labor
    d   would have gone to Esau had Esau not sold his birthright

73. **Jacob spent his wedding night with his bride's sister because**   [Genesis 29:16–23]
    a   their father palmed her off on him in the dark
    b   the Lord had foretold that his bride would be barren
    c   they were identical twins
    d   the bride palmed her off on him in the dark

74. **Jacob was persuaded to lie with**   [Genesis 30:1–4]
    a   Leah's maid Zilpah, by Rachel

b   Rachel's maid Bilhah, by Rachel
c   Rachel's maid Bilhah, by Leah
d   Leah, by Rachel

75. **Rachel escaped discovery and death for stealing her father's household gods because**   [Genesis 31:30, 34–35]
a   the night was pitch dark
b   she was in her monthly period
c   Jacob was forty-seven years of age
d   five camels were restive

76. **Israel became halt because**   [Genesis 32:24–31]
a   the stone that Esau cast at Rachel missed its mark
b   the presents for Esau were too heavy
c   God had touched the hollow of his thigh
d   of a congenital defect

77. **Jacob's sons Simeon and Levi took vengeance on the Hivites, for the rape of their sister Dinah, by**   [Genesis 34:13–26]
a   slaughter, taking them by surprise while sore from circumcision
b   driving the Hivite flocks into quicksands
c   loosening on all the Hivite cities a terror from God
d   ostracizing them

78. **Deborah was Dinah's**   [Genesis 35:8; 24:15, 29; 29:16; 30:20–21]
a   sister's uncle's nurse's daughter
b   mother's father's sister's nurse
c   nurse's sister's uncle's aunt
d   nurse's mother's cousin's daughter

79. **Jacob's four wives bore him**   [Genesis 35:22–26; 30:21]
a   twelve daughters and one son
b   twelve sons and no daughter
c   two daughters and eleven sons
d   one daughter and twelve sons

80. **Jacob's firstborn was**   [Genesis 35:23]
a   Joseph
b   Dan
c   Gad
d   Reuben

81. **Joseph's brothers plotted to kill him because**   [Genesis 37:5–11, 19–20]
a   they had dreamed of dominance over him
b   he had dreamed of dominance over them
c   their father had dreamed of his dominance over them
d   they were being tempted by Satan to sell him to the Ishmaelites for twenty shekels of silver

82. **The two brothers of Joseph that persuaded the others not to kill him were sons of Jacob's**   [Genesis 37:21–22, 26–27; 29:32, 35]

a first wife, Leah
b second wife, Bilhah
c third wife, Zilpah
d fourth wife, Rachel

83. **Joseph's brothers showed to their father his coat, which they had dipped in the blood of** [Genesis 37: 31–32]
a a sheep
b a wild beast
c themselves
d a kid

84. **Onan spilled his semen on the ground instead of impregnating Tamar because** [Genesis 38:8–9]
a he feared she was diseased
b the Lord had threatened him with impotence if he tried thus to take his brother's place
c the offspring would be regarded as his brother's, not his
d he desired to show disdain for Tamar

85. **Judah discovered he had had sexual relations with his daughter-in-law Tamar when** [Genesis 38:13–26]
a having ordered her burned for harlotry, he received from her a signet, bracelets, and a staff
b she gave birth to a child with a scarlet thread on his hand, who resembled Judah
c it grew light toward morning
d she told Shelah

86. **Joseph was imprisoned by the Egyptian captain of the guard, Potiphar, because Potiphar's wife accused Joseph of insulting her by** [Genesis 39:1, 7, 14–20]
a attempting to lie with her
b refusing to lie with her
c lying about her
d commenting on her relations with the members of the guard

87. **Joseph's first attempt at interpretations of dreams proved immediately encouraging from the viewpoint of**
[Genesis 40:12–13, 21]
a the butler
b the baker
c Joseph
d Benjamin

88. **The fact that Pharaoh dreamt doubly, of kine and ears, was said by Joseph to indicate that** [Genesis 41:32]
a there would be two cycles of plenty and famine
b God was testing Pharaoh's ability to select the correct dream for guidance
c God's mind was made up
d Pharaoh had eaten too large a supper

89. **Joseph imprisoned his ten grain-seeking brothers as alleged spies against Egypt because he** [Genesis 42:8–9; 37:5–11]
    a   recalled his dream of the sheaves and stars that made obeisance
    b   failed to recognize them
    c   was angry that they failed to recognize him
    d   had clear evidence

90. **In Joseph's conversation with his Hebrew-speaking brothers,** [Genesis 42:23]
    a   Joseph needed an interpreter to understand them
    b   they needed an interpreter to understand him
    c   no interpreter was needed
    d   two interpreters were needed

91. **The brother left behind as hostage when nine returned home to fetch Benjamin to Egypt was, of the twelve, the** [Genesis 42:24; 29:33]
    a   youngest
    b   next to the youngest
    c   oldest
    d   next to the oldest

92. **At the time Joseph's brothers came to Egypt the seven-year famine had been under way** [Genesis 45:6]
    a   one year
    b   two years
    c   five years
    d   six years

93. **Pharaoh issued to Joseph's brothers, their households, and his father** [Genesis 45:17–20]
    a   an engraved invitation
    b   a lukewarm invitation
    c   an ungracious invitation
    d   a command invitation

94. **Muppim, Huppim and Ard were** [Genesis 46:21]
    a   the closing words of the Egyptian prayer for victory
    b   three sons of Benjamin
    c   three rivers crossed on the journey to Egypt
    d   characters in a nursery rhyme

95. **As the famine years continued in Egypt, Joseph, acting for Pharaoh, distributed the grain he had hoarded in the good years** [Genesis 47:13–26]
    a   as payment in kind for labor on public works projects
    b   in return for the Egyptians' money, then their cattle, then their lands and themselves
    c   free of charge, but rationed according to individual needs
    d   through a lottery system

96. **The land of Goshen referred to in Genesis 47 was** [Genesis 47:27]

    a   between Canaan and Egypt
    b   in Canaan
    c   in Egypt
    d   what is now the island of Malta

97. **In blessing each of his twelve sons on his deathbed, Jacob likened**   [Genesis 49:3–27]
    a   Benjamin to a ravenous wolf
    b   Zebulun to a strong ass
    c   Joseph to a lion's whelp
    d   Dan to a fruitful bough

Exodus

98. **The new king of Egypt set taskmasters over the Israelites to afflict them with burdens because the Israelites**
    [Exodus 1:8–11]
    a   were so few that they were easily oppressed
    b   were converting so many Egyptians to their faith
    c   were so many and so mighty and could be a danger in time of war
    d   formed a hard core of unemployed and so were disaffected

99. **The Hebrew midwives did not kill Hebrew male children as ordered by the King of Egypt because**
    [Exodus 1:15–19]
    a   the Hebrew women were so lively that they were delivered before the midwives reached them
    b   they feared God
    c   at least two Hebrew men accompanied each midwife
    d   they misunderstood the order

100. **The child found by Pharaoh's daughter in the ark of bulrushes was thereafter nursed by**   [Exodus 2:7–9]
    a   Pharaoh's daughter
    b   the infant's sister
    c   the infant's mother
    d   one of Pharaoh's daughter's maidens

101. **The name Moses means**   [Exodus 2:10]
    a   drawn out of the water
    b   found in a basket of bulrushes
    c   found among the reeds
    d   coincidence

102. **Moses fled from Egypt because**   [Exodus 2:11-15]
    a he had killed an Egyptian
    b an Egyptian had wounded him
    c another Hebrew had killed an Egyptian
    d two Hebrews had killed one another

103. **Zipporah was the**   [Exodus 2:21-22]
    a place to which Moses fled
    b woman who bore Moses a child
    c place from which Moses fled
    d child the woman bore him

104. **Upon coming on the bush that was burning, yet not consumed, Moses' first reaction was to**   [Exodus 3:2-3]
    a avert his face
    b take a closer look
    c run away
    d pick it up

105. **God told Moses that when the Israelites finally succeeded in leaving Egypt they would**   [Exodus 3:21-22]
    a take with them all their possessions
    b leave all their possessions to the Egyptians
    c sell what they could and take the rest
    d spoil the Egyptians

106. **Aaron, not Moses, did the signs before the elders of Israel because**   [Exodus 4:1-16, 27-30]
    a Moses was diffident
    b the Lord was punishing Moses for disobedience
    c the elders knew that Moses had murdered
    d Aaron claimed he needed the practice

107. **The first mention of circumcision in Exodus is that of**
[Exodus 4:24-26; 2:21-22]
    a Aaron's son
    b Moses' son
    c Moses
    d Aaron's daughter

108. **"Let my people go" meant**   [Exodus 5:1, 3]
    a let them leave Egypt for the land of Canaan
    b free them from the bonds of slavery
    c allow them a few days off for a feast in the wilderness
    d permit them to cross and recross the border without a passport

109. **Pharaoh told the taskmasters and their officers that henceforth the Hebrews were to**   [Exodus 5:6-7]
    a make bricks without straw
    b make straw without bricks
    c make more bricks with less straw
    d gather their own straw

110. **Moses' father and mother were**   [Exodus 6:20]

      a   nephew and aunt
      b   uncle and niece
      c   half brother and sister
      d   cousins on the father's side

111. **When Moses and Aaron worked their miracles before Pharaoh they were**   [Exodus 7:7]
      a   under 40 years of age
      b   between 40 and 70
      c   between 70 and 110
      d   between 110 and 137

112. **Pharaoh's magicians matched Moses with**
                              [Exodus 7:10–12, 19–22; 8:5–7]
      a   lice, flies, frogs
      b   serpents, frogs, lice
      c   river blood, serpents, frogs
      d   serpents, river blood, lice

113. **The identifying blood of the passover lamb on Israelite houses was struck on the**   [Exodus 12:1, 7, 22]
      a   lintel and the two side posts
      b   two side posts and the mullion
      c   mullion and the two stiles
      d   two rails and the lintel

114. **The passover was so designated to mark the fact that the**   [Exodus 12:13]
      a   Israelites passed over the boundaries of Egypt on the exodus from that land
      b   Lord passed over the Egyptians, killing their first-born
      c   Lord spared the Israelites by passing over them
      d   Israelites went through a mountain pass on the exodus

115. **When the Israelites were thrust out of Egypt they carried with them**   [Exodus 12:35–36]
      a   none of their own possessions
      b   only their jewelry of silver and gold and their raiment
      c   silver and gold filched from the palace of Pharaoh
      d   jewelry of silver and gold and raiment freely lent them by the Egyptians

116. **The number of Israelites in the exodus was probably**
                              [Exodus 12:37]
      a   between 600,000 and 1,000,000
      b   between 1,000,000 and 5,000,000
      c   between 5,000,000 and 10,000,000
      d   under 600,000

117. **The Israelites had been in Egypt**   [Exodus 12:40]
      a   320 years
      b   430 years

    c   670 years
    d   830 years

118. **On the way to the land of the Canaanites, the Hittites, the Amorites, the Hivites and the Jebusites, God led the Israelites over the Red Sea rather than through the land of the Philistines**   [Exodus 13:5, 17–18]
    a   because it was the shorter route
    b   lest the Israelites see war and return to Egypt
    c   because he feared corruption by the Philistines
    d   for no specified reason

119. **The Lord went before the Israelites in a pillar of fire by night, to supply**   [Exodus 13:21]
    a   illumination
    b   protection
    c   consternation
    d   diversion

120. **The Lord drove the Red Sea back to provide passage for the Israelites by a strong wind from the**   [Exodus 14:21]
    a   east
    b   west
    c   north
    d   southwest

121. **When the waters of the Red Sea closed over the pursuing Egyptians, there survived**   [Exodus 14:28]
    a   not one of them
    b   all the firstborn, to compensate for the former slaughter
    c   all descendants of the chief butler who had put Joseph in touch with Pharaoh
    d   Pharaoh

122. **At Marah, where Moses cast into the water the tree that the Lord showed him,**   [Exodus 15:23–25]
    a   the tree took root, flourished, and provided shelter
    b   the Israelites hollowed out the trunk for a boat
    c   nothing happened
    d   the bitter water became sweet

123. **When the Israelites reached Sin they had been gone from Egypt**   [Exodus 16:1]
    a   half a month
    b   a month
    c   a month and a half
    d   two months

124. **The manna supplied by the Lord was**
    [Exodus 16:14–17]
    a   picked up off the ground
    b   picked off bushes
    c   picked off trees
    d   eaten as it fell

125. **On the sixth day of gathering the manna, twice as much appeared,** [Exodus 16:22–27]
    a as reserve for the journey ahead
    b because no manna would appear on the sabbath
    c because yesterday's manna had bred worms, and stank
    d because the Israelites had praised its taste, like wafers made with honey

126. **Moses smote the rock at Horeb because his people needed water for** [Exodus 17:1–6]
    a drinking
    b irrigation
    c washing
    d a religious ceremony

127. **Amalek would have gained the battle with the Israelites had not Aaron and Hur held up Moses'**
    [Exodus 17:11–13]
    a hands
    b arms
    c legs
    d body

128. **The great contribution made by Moses' father-in-law was to tell him how to** [Exodus 18:13–26]
    a find his way out of the wilderness
    b formulate the ordinances for the Ten Commandments
    c decentralize his authority
    d select his successor

129. **To the Israelites encamped at the foot of Mt. Sinai the Lord appeared in the form of** [Exodus 19:2, 9, 16; 20:21]
    a a burning bush
    b an earthquake
    c a thick cloud
    d a pillar of fire

130. **The commandments forbade certain actions specifically against one's neighbor in** [Exodus 20:16–17]
    a one commandment
    b two commandments
    c three commandments
    d four commandments

131. **By the Lord's ordinances, a master was to bore a Hebrew servant's ear through with an aul when**
    [Exodus 21:5–6]
    a a servant renounced his chance for freedom
    b a runaway servant was recaptured
    c a servant renounced his religion
    d two servants were identical twins

132. **The ordinances decreed the death penalty for anyone who**
    [Exodus 21:17]

a   cursed his father or mother
b   spat on his mother
c   stole from his father
d   betrayed his father to his mother

133. **The dictum of an eye for an eye, a tooth for a tooth (and so on) was first promulgated by the Lord in the ordinance dealing with**   [Exodus 21:22–25]
a   miscarriage
b   revenge
c   servants
d   money lending

134. **The ordinances did not extend the "eye for eye" rule to**
[Exodus 21:23–25]
a   hand for hand
b   foot for foot
c   ear for ear
d   stripe for stripe

135. **If a man stole an ox, ass, or a sheep, he had to restore double if the beast was found**   [Exodus 22:4]
a   alive in his possession
b   dead in his possession
c   alive in the hands of others
d   dead in the hands of others

136. **A man who seduced an unbetrothed maid would be compelled to marry her**   [Exodus 22:16–17]
a   under all circumstances
b   under no circumstances
c   under one circumstance
d   except under one circumstance

137. **The ordinances imposed the death penalty for**
[Exodus 22:19]
a   sodding
b   bestiality
c   estrepement
d   pederasty

138. **A loan to another Israelite who was poor had to be made at**   [Exodus 22:25]
a   zero interest
b   negative interest
c   not more than 6 percent
d   no higher than the market rate

139. **To make room for the Israelites, the Lord said He would drive out the Hivites, Canaanites and Hittites only little by little, to assure**
[Exodus 23:28–31; see also Deuteronomy 7:22]
a   justice to these peoples
b   time to resettle them in Egypt

    c   that the land would not become desolate
    d   enough servants for the Israelites

140. **The Lord instructed Moses to place the mercy seat**
                                       [Exodus 25:21]
    a   on the ark
    b   beneath the ark
    c   in the ark
    d   five feet from the ark

141. **The Lord directed each Israelite counted in the census
to give an offering to the Lord, the amount to be**
                                    [Exodus 30:12–15]
    a   half a shekel if rich, half a shekel if poor
    b   half a shekel if rich, a shekel if poor
    c   a shekel if rich, half a shekel if poor
    d   two shekels if rich, half a shekel if poor

142. **The Israelites were saved from destruction by the Lord
when they had worshiped the molten calf made by Aaron
from their earrings only because**   [Exodus 32:1–14]
    a   they repented
    b   the Lord repented
    c   Moses repented
    d   Aaron repented

143. **The tables, on which God had graven the commandments, and which Moses carried down from the mountain, were**   [Exodus 32:15–16]
    a   two, each written on on both sides
    b   two, each written on on one side
    c   three, each written on on one side
    d   ten, each containing one commandment

144. **Moses broke the Ten Commandments**   [Exodus 32:19]
    a   in spirit
    b   abstractly
    c   metaphorically
    d   in pieces

145. **Moses was so angry when he saw his people worshiping
the molten calf that he made them**   [Exodus 32:20]
    a   chew it
    b   drink it
    c   wear it
    d   break it

146. **Aaron's explanation to Moses of how the molten calf
came to be was**   [Exodus 32:22–24, 2–4]
    a   disingenuous
    b   ingenious
    c   ingenuous
    d   contentious

147. **The cloudy pillar that descended and stood at the door**

whenever Moses went into the tabernacle was a sign that
the Lord was   [Exodus 33:9–11]
a threatening Moses
b silently observing Moses
c guarding Moses from intrusion
d speaking to Moses face to face, as a man speaks to
   his friend

148. **The Lord proposed to put Moses in a clift of a rock in
     order that**   [Exodus 33:21–23]
     a he might see only the back of the Lord
     b he might be protected from his fellow Israelites
     c he might strike the rock to bring forth water
     d Aaron would not be able to find him

149. **The census taken of the Israelites (No. 141) showed the
     number of men twenty or more years of age to be**
                                                 [Exodus 38:26]
     a 60,355
     b 603,550
     c 6,035,500
     d under 60,355

Leviticus

150. **One who obtained something by lying about what was
     deposited with him for safekeeping, or what he had
     found (lost by another), or by violence, or deceit was to
     restore it to its owner, plus**   [Leviticus 6:1–5]
     a a fifth of its value
     b one-half its value
     c double its value
     d varying proportions, depending on the offense

151. **When Moses performed the ceremony that made Aaron
     and his sons the priests of Israel, he**
                            [Leviticus 8:5–29; Exodus 29:4–28]
     a betrayed pique that the priesthood was not his
     b demonstrated a remarkable memory for detail
     c required them to remake and destroy a molten calf
     d forbade other Israelites to lay claim to the priesthood

152. **Two of Aaron's sons put fire in their censers, with in-
     cense, and for this they were**   [Leviticus 10:1–2]
     a rebuked by Moses

    b   rebuked by Aaron
    c   burned to death by the Lord
    d   praised by Moses and Aaron

153. **The hare and the camel were alike forbidden to the Israelites for food because** [Leviticus 11:3–8]
    a   although both of them chew the cud, neither of them parts the hoof
    b   both chew the cud
    c   both part the hoof
    d   neither one chews the cud or parts the hoof

154. **Of the living things in the seas and rivers, the Israelites were allowed to eat only those with** [Leviticus 11:9–12]
    a   both fins and scales
    b   fins
    c   scales
    d   neither fins nor scales

155. **Among the birds specifically forbidden to the Israelites for food were** [Leviticus 11:13–19]
    a   raven, ostrich, swallow, pelican
    b   eagle, ossifrage, owl, pelican
    c   kite, cormorant, vulture, motmot
    d   osprey, sea gull, water hen, kingfisher

156. **The "flying creeping" things "that goeth upon all four" permitted to the Israelites for food were those with**
    [Leviticus 11:20–23]
    a   legs above their feet
    b   no legs above their feet
    c   no legs or feet
    d   feet above their legs

157. **A leper, decreed the Lord, must cover his**
    [Leviticus 13:45]
    a   face
    b   head
    c   forehead
    d   upper lip

158. **The animal designated by the Lord to bear the iniquities of the people of Israel and go thus laden into the wilderness was** [Leviticus 16:22]
    a   a ram
    b   an ox
    c   a goat
    d   a bull

159. **The Lord prohibited the Israelites from eating any manner of blood because** [Leviticus 17:10–14]
    a   atonement for their souls was to be made through the animal's blood on the altar
    b   blood in the diet induced ferocity in the spirit

    c   the rich would be tempted to induce the poor to
        donate blood
    d   it made an unsightly dish

160. **The Lord's instructions to Moses in Leviticus 18 and 20
forbidding any Israelite from "uncovering the nakedness"
of his relatives happened not specifically to mention
among those relatives one's** [Leviticus 18:7–18; 20:10–21]
    a   mother
    b   daughter
    c   sister
    d   aunt

161. **The Lord's instructions to Moses in Leviticus 18 and 20
happened not to include specifically a prohibition against
sexual relations of** [Leviticus 18:20–23; 20:10–21]
    a   man with man
    b   woman with woman
    c   man with animal
    d   man with neighbor's wife

162. **In Leviticus the Lord enjoined each Israelite to love as
himself** [Leviticus 19:18, 34]
    a   only a stranger dwelling with him
    b   only his neighbor
    c   both his neighbor and a stranger dwelling with him
    d   all mankind

163. **If a man lay with his uncle's wife, the penalty for this
was to** [Leviticus 20:20]
    a   be put to death
    b   be exiled
    c   die childless
    d   be ostracized

164. **The Israelite priests were forbidden to** [Leviticus 21:5]
    a   make their heads bald
    b   wear beards
    c   round off the hair on their temples
    d   part their hair on the left side

165. **When an Israelite reaped the harvest of his land, he was
not to make clean riddance of the corners, because something should be left for** [Leviticus 23:22]
    a   wildlife
    b   the poor and the stranger
    c   the Lord
    d   those who were to be driven out gradually

166. **The Lord ordered that on the day of atonement (the
tenth day of the seventh month) the Israelites should**
[Leviticus 23:27–28]
    a   work twice as long as usual
    b   work 50 percent longer than usual
    c   work as usual
    d   not work at all

167. **In dealing with the case of the Shelomith's son, the Lord extended the eye-for-an-eye doctrine (Nos. 133, 134 above) to:**   [Leviticus 24:20]
    a   ear for ear
    b   cut for cut
    c   breach for breach
    d   toe for toe

168. **The year of Jubilee was to be every**   [Leviticus 25:10]
    a   seventh year
    b   fourteenth year
    c   fiftieth year
    d   one hundredth year

169. **The Lord promised that every sixth year He would cause the land to yield enough to supply the Israelites for**
                                                    [Leviticus 25:20–22]
    a   one year
    b   two years
    c   three years
    d   four years

170. **Under the Lord's property laws, property sold was to revert to the seller in the year of Jubilee, if it was**
                        [Leviticus 25:23, 29–34, 39–41, 44–46]
    a   a dwelling house in a walled city sold by a non-Levite
    b   an Israelite who had sold himself as a servant
    c   a non-Israelite whom an Israelite had purchased as a servant
    d   a parcel of land sold in perpetuity

171. **If the following four of the many punishments by which the Lord threatened the Israelites for disobedience are numbered**
        (1) pestilence in their cities, (2) causing them to eat the flesh of their sons and daughters, (3) terror, consumption and the burning ague consuming their eyes and causing sorrow of heart, (4) wild beasts robbing them of their children and destroying their cattle, the order in which they were to be successively applied was
                                                    [Leviticus 26:14–29]
    a   (1), (2), (3), (4)
    b   (4), (3), (1), (2)
    c   (4), (1), (2), (3)
    d   (3), (4), (1), (2)

Numbers

172. **Of the twelve sons of Jacob the census was not taken of the tribe of** [Numbers 1:47]
    a Gad
    b Zebulun
    c Judah
    d Levi

173. **The tribe of Levi was given by the Lord to Aaron for assistance in religious ceremonies** [Numbers 3:6–12]
    a as the largest of the tribes
    b as the smallest of the tribes
    c in substitution for every firstborn of all the tribes
    d after a fervent request by Levi

174. **"The Lord bless thee, and keep thee; . . . The Lord lift up his countenance upon thee, and give thee peace" was to be said** [Numbers 6:22–26]
    a to an Israelite when the time of his separation as a Nazarite was completed
    b to an Israelite at the time of making the special vow of the Nazarite
    c by the Nazarite to his fellow Israelites
    d by Moses to Aaron and his sons

175. **As long as the cloud rested over the tabernacle, this was the Lord's sign to the Israelite hosts to** [Numbers 9:15–23]
    a keep going
    b pray
    c stay
    d eat

176. **Some of the Israelites incurred the Lord's wrath by developing a craving for** [Numbers 11:4]
    a flesh
    b manna
    c liquor
    d tobacco

177. **Eldad and Medad were immortalized with a few lines in the Old Testament because they** [Numbers 11:26–29]
    a were the first Siamese twins born during the long march
    b prophesied in the camp instead of in the tabernacle
    c attempted to seize the priestly power from Aaron
    d spied out the promised land, from Zin to Rehob

178. **The Lord satisfied the Israelites' craving for flesh, but at the same time He** [Numbers 11:31-34]
   a smote them
   b redeemed them
   c forgave them
   d received their repentance

179. **When Aaron's sister Miriam was made leprous because she and Aaron had angered the Lord by doubting that He spoke through Moses alone, He relented after**
[Numbers 12:1-2, 10-15]
   a Aaron had beseeched the Lord
   b Aaron had beseeched Moses
   c Aaron had beseeched Moses and Moses had beseeched the Lord
   d Miriam had beseeched the Lord

180. **The Lord set the period for the Israelites' children to wander in the wilderness at just forty years because**
[Numbers 14:33-34]
   a forty was a favorite number of the Lord's
   b the Israelite scouts had spent forty days pessimistically searching the promised land
   c no Israelite over forty would live to inhabit the promised land
   d Moses persuaded Him to reduce it from eighty years

181. **Having found a man gathering sticks on the Sabbath day, the Israelites inquired of the Lord and meted out the punishment He demanded, namely,** [Numbers 15:32-36]
   a replacement of each stick just where it had been gathered
   b payment of forty shekels to the tabernacle
   c carrying the sticks until he gained the promised land
   d death by stoning

182. **Fourteen thousand seven hundred Israelites perished under the Lord's wrath when they were**
[Numbers 16:49]
   a swallowed up as the earth split asunder
   b consumed by fire
   c struck by the plague
   d wandering lost in the wilderness

183. **Aaron and his descendants, decreed the Lord, should receive in partial recompense for their religious duties**
[Numbers 18:26-28]
   a the tithe
   b a tithe of the tithe
   c a tithe of a tithe of the tithe
   d none of the tithe

184. **When Aaron died on mount Hor by the Lord's command, all the house of Israel wept for him**
[Numbers 20:27-29]

    a   ten days
    b   twenty days
    c   thirty days
    d   forty days

185. **Balaam's ass**   [Numbers 22:21–33]
    a   brought him into disfavor with the Lord
    b   delayed his journey by stupid indecision
    c   saved his life
    d   rolled on him

186. **"What hath God wrought!" was the exclamation**
                                [Numbers 23:16–23]
    a   by Balaam, when he blessed the people of Israel before Balak
    b   by Moses, when he struck a rock in Moab to obtain water
    c   by Aaron, just before he died
    d   in the Book of the Wars of the Lord

187. **Of the 603,550 men who had been counted in the Sinai wilderness census by Moses and Aaron, there remained to be counted by Moses and Eleazar, in the census taken after the plague,**   [Numbers 26:1, 63–65; 1:46]
    a   207,463
    b   2,075
    c   2
    d   none

188. **The appeal by the women Mahlah, Noah, Hoglah, Milcah and Tirzah stimulated the Lord to decree the order of inheritance if there were no sons:**   [Numbers 27:1–11]
    a   daughter, (if no daughter) brother, (if no brother) sister, (if no sister) uncle (on father's side)
    b   brother, daughter, sister, uncle
    c   daughter, brother, sister, next of kin
    d   daughter, brother, uncle, next of kin

189. **Having notified Moses that he was about to die, the Lord heeded his request to nominate a successor to shepherd Israel, and named**   [Numbers 27:13–23]
    a   Joshua
    b   Eleazar
    c   Zelophehad
    d   Nun

190. **The Lord decreed that when a woman vows a vow to the Lord and binds herself by a bond it is binding on her only if her husband (or her father, if she is unmarried) hears it and**   [Numbers 30:3–15]
    a   says nothing
    b   expresses his approval
    c   expresses his disapproval
    d   signs as a witness

191. **When the Israelite army returned, having killed every Midianite adult male, Moses was angry and commanded them to**   [Numbers 31:7–18]
    a   indemnify the widows of Midianite prisoners slain by them
    b   pass to the Levites all their booty of gold and silver
    c   kill more: every male child and every woman not a virgin, keeping the young girl virgins alive for themselves
    d   seek other foes to test their courage

192. **The booty from the Midian war, divided equally between those who fought and all the children of Israel, was taxed for the Lord: warriors' share and children of Israel's share, respectively, at**   [Numbers 31:27–30]
    a   10 percent and 5 percent
    b   10 percent and 33 1/3 percent
    c   2 percent and 1 percent
    d   one-fifth of 1 percent and 2 percent

193. **The boundaries of the land of Canaan which the Israelites were to possess were, by the Lord,**
                                            [Numbers 34:1–12]
    a   described precisely
    b   not mentioned
    c   sketched vaguely
    d   submitted to binding arbitration

194. **Six cities, to be designated cities for refuge, in the new land were to serve as places to which there might flee for safety any**   [Numbers 35:6, 9–12]
    a   Israelite threatened with harm by a fellow Israelite
    b   one who killed by accident
    c   Canaanite refugees
    d   Levite

195. **The Lord decreed that no alleged murderer should be put to death on the testimony of**   [Numbers 35:30]
    a   priests alone
    b   strangers alone
    c   one witness alone
    d   relatives alone

196. **Mahlah, Noah, Hoglah, Milcah and Tirzah (No. 188 above) were commanded by Moses to marry within their tribe, in order that**   [Numbers 36:6–9]
    a   the purity of Joseph's tribe might be maintained
    b   their conduct might not demoralize other tribes
    c   they might be punished for complaining about the laws of succession
    d   no inheritance should be transferred from one tribe to another

Deuteronomy

197. **The first four chapters of the Fifth Book of Moses contain a summary of the** [Deuteronomy 1–4]
a laws handed down by the Lord through Moses
b ordinances
c forty years in the wilderness
d genealogy of the tribes of Israel

198. **Moses was allowed by the Lord to**
[Deuteronomy 3:25–27]
a enter the good land beyond the Jordan
b enter Lebanon
c go to the Jordan
d go only to Bashan

199. **The Lord forbade intermarriage with nations being dispossessed, fearing** [Deuteronomy 7:3–4]
a entangled inheritances
b language difficulties
c induced apostasy
d Egyptian violence

200. **When the Lord was making the Israelites know that man does not live by bread only, He was** [Deuteronomy 8:3]
a supplying them with manna
b depriving them of manna
c promising them manna
d supplementing bread with manna

201. **If an Israelite's brother, or son, or daughter, or wife, or close friend, were to entice him secretly to serve other gods, he should, says Deuteronomy 13,**
[Deuteronomy 13:6–10]
a kill the enticer
b persuade the enticer to desist
c leave the enticer
d ostracize the enticer

202. **At the end of every seven years every Israelite creditor was to** [Deuteronomy 15:1–3]
a release all his debtors
b release all his Israelite debtors
c extend each debt another seven years if requested
d adjust the debt according to the cost-of-living index

203. **At a time when the seventh year, the year of release,**

was near, lenders were to accede to a poor Israelite's request by lending to him   [Deuteronomy 15:7-11]

a freely
b only if he was certain to repay before that year
c only after that year had passed
d at double the usual rate of interest

204. **The point of eating unleavened bread with the passover
sacrifice was, among other things, that**
                                  [Deuteronomy 16:1-3]

a yeast was an unclean food
b it was a mild form of penance
c unleavened bread, less bulky, was easier to pack
d the Israelites might thereby remember the day when
   they had come out of Egypt in haste

205. **An image, declared Moses to the Israelites, the Lord
thy God**   [Deuteronomy 16:22]
a hateth
b loveth
c ignoreth
d noteth

206. **No one could be stoned to death, declared Moses, for
serving and worshiping other gods without evidence from
at least**   [Deuteronomy 17:2-6]
a one witness
b two witnesses
c three witnesses
d twelve witnesses

207. **The Lord was dispossessing the nations of the lands He
was turning over to the Israelites because they**
                                  [Deuteronomy 18:10-14]
a had defied His orders to leave
b had given heed to enchanters, witches, charmers,
   wizards, necromancers, and the like
c had taken these lands from ancestors of the Israelites
d were being recompensed by the Lord with still
   better lands elsewhere

208. **Deuteronomy 19 says that no charge concerning any
iniquity or sin was to be sustained without evidence
from at least**   [Deuteronomy 19:15]
a one witness
b two witnesses
c three witnesses
d four witnesses

209. **Not excused from the battlefront were those Israelites
who had**   [Deuteronomy 20:5-9]
a built a new house and not dedicated it
b planted a vineyard and not eaten of it
c betrothed a wife and not taken her
d dug a new well and not drunk of it

210. **A warrior could pick a beautiful woman from among the captives to be his wife but could not lie with her until** [Deuteronomy 21:10–13]
   a   he was certain that no other captive was her husband
   b   she had kept his house for a month and proved herself clean
   c   she had stayed in his house a month bewailing her father and mother
   d   she invited him to

211. **If the husband then had no delight in his wife he** [Deuteronomy 21:14]
   a   could sell her to the highest bidder
   b   had to let her go where she would
   c   could keep her as his wife only until the seventh year
   d   had to find another husband for her

212. **The firstborn of a man with two wives, one loved, the other hated, was entitled to the usual double portion of the firstborn** [Deuteronomy 21:15–17]
   a   whether he was the son of the loved or the hated
   b   only if he was the son of the loved
   c   only if he was the son of the hated
   d   in neither case

213. **A stubborn and rebellious son, refusing to obey his father and his mother even after they had chastened him, was to be** [Deuteronomy 21:18–21]
   a   disinherited
   b   imprisoned for one year
   c   exiled
   d   stoned to death

214. **Upon coming across a lost ox, sheep, ass, or raiment, an Israelite was to** [Deuteronomy 22:1–3]
   a   leave it strictly alone
   b   take it to the nearest Levite
   c   take it to its owner or hold it at home until the owner was found
   d   take it and sell it

215. **Transvestism was, to the Lord,** [Deuteronomy 22:5]
   a   a matter of no concern
   b   laughable
   c   understandable
   d   an abomination

216. **Every new house was to have a battlement for the roof, to** [Deuteronomy 22:8]
   a   provide cover for repelling marauders
   b   provide shade for the siesta
   c   avert falls from the roof
   d   signify Israelite unity

217. **Wearing a garment of divers sorts, as of woollen and linen together, was** [Deuteronomy 22:11]
    a prohibited
    b ridiculed
    c encouraged
    d not mentioned

218. **Whether a young woman, accused by her husband of not having been a virgin, was or was not able to show the tokens of virginity was a matter**
    [Deuteronomy 22:13–21]
    a of indifference to the Israelite community at large
    b to be settled somehow by a money payment
    c of grave concern, involving possible exile
    d of life or death

219. **If a man was found to be lying with another's wife**
    [Deuteronomy 22:22]
    a the woman was to be divorced and the man was to marry her
    b the man was to die
    c the woman was to die
    d both were to die

220. **Punishment for rape of a virgin was to be either**
    [Deuteronomy 22:25–29]
    a death or exile
    b exile or money indemnity
    c death or money indemnity and marriage
    d money indemnity or marriage

221. **The congregation of the Lord was not to be barred to**
    [Deuteronomy 23:1–8]
    a Ammonites or Moabites
    b an Israelite wounded in the stones or whose privy member had been cut off
    c a bastard
    d a fourth-generation Egyptian

222. **Every Israelite warrior was to carry a paddle upon his weapon, so that he might** [Deuteronomy 23:12–14]
    a signal for help
    b start a fire
    c cover up his excrement
    d limp home if wounded

223. **An Israelite was not forbidden to**
    [Deuteronomy 23:24–25]
    a eat his fill of grapes in his neighbor's vineyard
    b put one or more grapes into his vessel
    c put a sickle to his neighbor's standing grain
    d do both b and c

224. **A man, whose former wife, after being divorced by him**

because of some uncleanness in her, married and was
again divorced or was widowed, was not to
[Deuteronomy 24:1–4]

a   refuse to remarry her
b   remarry her
c   marry her to someone else
d   send her into exile

225. **A newly married man was to be free from going out
with the army or being charged with any business for
one**   [Deuteronomy 24:5]

a   day
b   week
c   month
d   year

226. **The Israelite was not specifically forbidden to**
[Deuteronomy 24:19–22]

a   go back to fetch a forgotten sheaf
b   go over the boughs of his olive trees after beating
    them
c   glean his vineyard after gathering its grapes
d   milk the cow after the first pail was full

227. **The guilty man in a dispute could be given by the judge
a maximum beating of**   [Deuteronomy 25:1–3]

a   ten stripes
b   twenty stripes
c   forty stripes
d   eighty stripes

228. **A childless widow of one who had been dwelling with
his brother was to pull her brother-in-law's shoe off his
foot and spit in his face if he**   [Deuteronomy 25:5–9]

a   asked her to marry him
b   refused to ask her to marry him
c   advised her never to marry anyone else
d   put her out of the house

229. **If the wife of one who was losing in a fight with another man tried to rescue him by seizing his opponent
by the secrets, she was to be**   [Deuteronomy 25:11–12]

a   commended
b   assisted
c   directed
d   punished

230. **Each Israelite was to have, of kinds of weights or measures,**   [Deuteronomy 25:13–16]

a   one
b   two
c   three
d   four

231. **The Lord did not promise, if the Israelites hearkened**

unto His voice and did all His commandments, that they
would   [Deuteronomy 28:1–14]
a live to a ripe old age
b lend to many nations but not borrow
c find all the people of the earth afraid of them
d be above only

232. And if they did not hearken to His voice, and do all
His commandments and statutes, the Lord did not promise that [Deuteronomy 28:15–68, especially 22, 23, 25]
a the heaven over their heads would be brass, and the
   earth under them, iron
b He would smite them with a consumption, a fever,
   an inflammation, an extreme burning, the sword,
   blasting, and mildew
c they would lose their hearing and sense of smell
d they would go out one way against their enemies
   and flee before them seven ways

233. He further, in that event, did not promise that
            [Deuteronomy 28:15–68, especially 27, 31, 43–44]
a He would smite them with the botch of Egypt, the
   emerods, the scab and the itch
b their oxen would be slain before their eyes and they
   would not eat of it
c all the males would become impotent
d the stranger among them would lend to them, and
   they would not lend to him

234. And finally He did not promise that
            [Deuteronomy 28:15–68, especially 53–55, 68]
a they would eat the flesh of their sons and daughters
b the tender and delicate man would refuse to give
   his starving wife any of the flesh of their children
   that he would be eating
c they would be sold to their enemies as bondmen and
   bondwomen but no man would buy them
d they would give birth to children physically deformed
   and mentally retarded

235. Shortly before Moses' death the Lord predicted that His
people afterward would   [Deuteronomy 31:16–17]
a desert the Lord, and thereupon be devoured
b faithfully worship the Lord and thereby prosper
c split into two groups, one of a, the other of b
d prove unpredictable

236. In the song that Moses wrote, "the apple of his eye"
refers to the eye of   [Deuteronomy 32:9–10; 31:30]
a Moses
b the Lord
c the Israelite nation collectively
d no one in particular

237. **In "to me belongeth vengeance," "me" refers to**
[Deuteronomy 32:19, 20, 35]
   a   the Lord
   b   Moses
   c   Joshua
   d   the Hittite King

238. **Moses saw the Promised Land from the mountain on which he died,**   [Deuteronomy 32:48–50; 34:1–5]
   a   mount Hor
   b   mount Sinai
   c   mount Nebo
   d   mount Paran

239. **Moses lived** [Deuteronomy 34:7; Genesis 5:5; see No. 23]
   a   more than twice as long as Adam
   b   half as long as Adam
   c   less than one-seventh as long as Adam
   d   an unstated number of years

Joshua

240. **The line of scarlet thread bound in the harlot Rahab's window in Jericho was**   [Joshua 2:1–21]
   a   a sign to clients
   b   a safeguard against slaughter
   c   a signal to attack
   d   an inconsequential decoration

241. **The twelve stones taken by the Israelites from the Jordan after they passed over toward Jericho**   [Joshua 4:1–10]
   a   had served as stepping stones for crossing the river
   b   came from the place where the priests had stood in the dry river bed
   c   had been hurled at them by the Hittites as they forded the river
   d   were used, one by each tribe, to shatter the walls of Jericho

242. **The Israelite children born during the forty years' wandering in the wilderness crossed the Jordan**
[Joshua 5:2–7]
   a   uncircumcised
   b   circumcised
   c   circumcised save for those under ten years of age
   d   perhaps circumcised, perhaps not

243. **After the crossing of the Jordan, the manna**
[Joshua 5:11–12]

    a   ceased
    b   continued as before
    c   redoubled
    d   improved in flavor

244. **The total number of times the Israelites marched around the walls of Jericho was** [Joshua 6:1–4]
    a   two
    b   seven
    c   thirteen
    d   forty-nine

245. **The second march around the walls of Jericho is reported in Joshua 6 to have been made**
[Joshua 6:12–14]
    a   in silence
    b   with blowing of trumpets
    c   with shouting and blowing of trumpets
    d   in casual conversation

246. **On the last march, with trumpets and shout, the walls of Jericho** [Joshua 6:20]
    a   exploded upward in small pieces
    b   fell down flat
    c   opened in seven wide breaches
    d   crumpled into hills of rubble

247. **Joshua's second attack on Ai succeeded, when the first had failed, fundamentally because**
[Joshua 7:1–26; 8:1–29]
    a   Joshua was gaining skill with practice
    b   he used 30,000 men instead of 3,000 men
    c   he invented the ambush
    d   the Lord had been placated by the death of Achan

248. **The inhabitants of Gibeon talked poor, and as their reward** [Joshua 9:3–27]
    a   received gifts of silver and gold
    b   became hewers of wood and drawers of water
    c   were wiped out to the last man
    d   were loaned money at zero interest

249. **The five kings of the Amorites had the misfortune to encounter a** [Joshua 10:5, 11]
    a   hailstorm
    b   rainstorm
    c   lightning
    d   hot, sticky weather

250. **The Israelites had to live with those who inhabited the one city from which they were unable to drive out the occupants; namely,** [Joshua 15:63; 10:28–32]
    a   Jerusalem
    b   Makkedah
    c   Libnah
    d   Lachish

251. **Shiloh was the place where**   [Joshua 18:1]
   a all the children of Israel assembled to set up the
      tabernacle when the land before them was subdued
   b the battle raged in which the Ephraimites defeated
      the Canaanites
   c the busiest river crossing of the Jordan was located
   d lots were cast for the inheritances of Mahlah, Noah,
      Hoglah, Milcah, and Tirzah

252. **The refugee to a city of refuge (No. 194 above) was to
   be allowed entrance**   [Joshua 20:4]
   a unconditionally
   b if he brought a certificate of good character from
      two of his fellow inhabitants
   c if he stopped at the city gate and explained his case
      to the elders
   d if he offered a ram in sacrifice

253. **The huge altar built by the Reubenites, the Gadites,
   and the half-tribe of Manasseh almost**   [Joshua 22:10–34]
   a bankrupted them
   b provoked a rash of huge altars
   c involved them in a hopeless war
   d fell down

254. **The great stone at Shechem was to serve as a witness
   against the Israelites if they betrayed the covenant they
   made with Joshua to serve the Lord, since the stone**
                                         [Joshua 24:1, 26–27]
   a had heard that covenant spoken
   b bore that covenant engraved upon it
   c faced in the direction of the covenanters' lands
   d covered the covenant

255. **Joshua's life, compared with Moses', was**
                           [Joshua 24:29; Deuteronomy 34:7]
   a longer
   b shorter
   c the same
   d unknown

Judges

256. **Adonibezek said seventy kings used to gather their
   meat under his table after he had cut off their**
                                               [Judges 1:7]

   a thumbs and great toes

    b   forefingers and great toes
    c   index fingers and forefingers
    d   thumbs and little fingers

257. **In the description of how Ehud the Benjamite delivered the Israelites from servitude to Eglon the King of Moab, it is emphasized that he was** [Judges 3:15–22]
    a   long legged
    b   left-handed
    c   color-blind
    d   keen-scented

258. **Deborah, the wife of Lapidoth, was a** [Judges 4:4–5]
    a   judge
    b   priest
    c   general
    d   quartermaster

259. **When Captain Sisera let the wife of Heber hide him under a mantle, he made** [Judges 4:2, 17–21]
    a   an astute move
    b   an uncomfortable choice
    c   a treacherous ploy
    d   a mistake

260. **When Gideon asked for proof of His authenticity, the Lord was** [Judges 6:13–22, 36–40]
    a   impatient
    b   patient
    c   baffled
    d   outraged

261. **The fleece and the dew was Gideon's test of**
[Judges 6:36–40]
    a   the Lord
    b   himself
    c   Asher, Zebulun, and Naphtali
    d   the Midianites

262. **The size of the army Gideon planned to throw at the Midianites made the Lord uneasy because** [Judges 7:2]
    a   if panic threatened, some part of the unwieldy body would give way
    b   Gideon might become conceited with too easy a victory
    c   He wanted the Israelites to lose
    d   the Israelites might believe they had won without His aid

263. **That a cake of barley bread tumbled into the host of Midian and overturned a tent was a dream of**
[Judges 7:13–15]
    a   Gideon's
    b   another Israelite's

    c   a Midianite's
    d   the Lord's

264. **When Gideon's trumpets sounded, the**   [Judges 7:19-22]
    a   walls of Jericho collapsed
    b   Midianites fought one another
    c   fearful and the trembling returned to do battle
    d   Lord was angered

265. **When Gideon asked bread for his followers from the men of Succoth, they**   [Judges 8:4-7]
    a   gave their help
    b   refused their help
    c   ignored his plea
    d   disagreed among themselves

266. **Abimelech was finally slain by**   [Judges 9:53-54]
    a   a man wielding a sword
    b   a woman throwing a millstone from a tower
    c   bundles of burning brush
    d   an ambush in the fields

267. **The daughter of Gilead's son Jephthah bewailed her virginity because**   [Judges 11:1, 30-40]
    a   she knew her father would give her for a burnt offering
    b   she had been trapped into vows to the Baals
    c   her true love had been slain at Minnith
    d   she was fearful of men

268. **"Shibboleth" was a**   [Judges 12:5-6]
    a   password
    b   good luck charm
    c   test of identity by pronunciation
    d   minor Syrian deity between the Baals and the Ashtaroth

269. **Samson's father-to-be, eager for more advice, persuaded the angel of the Lord to make a second visit,**
                                                    [Judges 13:2-14, 24]
    a   but on that score he might as well have spared himself this trouble
    b   and obtained invaluable suggestions on how to raise the forthcoming child
    c   but was rebuked for his importuning
    d   and enhanced his standing by inviting all the neighbors

270. **The Lord started Samson on his fights with the Philistines by**   [Judges 14:1-4]
    a   giving him the jawbone of an ass
    b   inciting them to slay his mother
    c   provoking them through his feats of strength
    d   causing him to become enamoured of a daughter of a Philistine

271. **Samson's wife betrayed him to her countrymen out of**
[Judges 14:15–18]

    a fear
    b love
    c hate
    d greed

272. **Samson wagered some Philistines that they could not answer his riddle, and Philistines**   [Judges 14:12–14, 19]

    a won the wager
    b lost the wager
    c won the wager and supplied the prize
    d never decided the wager

273. **Samson destroyed the Philistines' shocks, standing corn, vineyards, and olives by using foxes that were**
[Judges 15:3–6]

    a ravenous
    b diseased
    c tied
    d vicious

274. **When the Philistines burned Samson's wife and father-in-law, he**   [Judges 15:6–8]

    a slaughtered them with the jawbone of an ass
    b thanked them for destroying a disloyal wife
    c pulled down upon them the walls of their city
    d smote them hip and thigh

275. **The cords and bands that were loosed from off Samson's arms and hands had been fastened on him**
[Judges 15:9–14]

    a with his consent
    b against his will
    c while he was asleep
    d while he was drugged with wine

276. **Samson was**   [Judges 15:20]
    a a judge of the Israelites
    b judged by an Israelite judge
    c a foe of judges
    d a judge *manqué*

277. **After sleeping with a harlot at Gaza, Samson**
[Judges 16:1–3]

    a pulled down the pillars of the temple
    b took away the doors of the city gate and the two posts
    c tossed the Gazites about as straw in the wind
    d left peacefully

278. **Samson told Delilah the true secret of his strength after he had seen her try to betray him**   [Judges 16:4–17]

    a once
    b twice

    c   three times

    d   not at all

279. **Samson lost his strength when the seven locks of his head were shaved off because** [Judges 16:17–20]

    a   his hair contained a chemical substance that increased oxygen use by his muscles

    b   a psychological connection existed in his mind between hairiness and strength

    c   since birth he had been a Nazarite to God

    d   blood poisoning from the unclean razor weakened him

280. **If the story of Micah and the Danites seems rather pointless, it is probably because** [Judges 17, 18]

    a   nothing dreadful befell either Micah or the Danites

    b   it only demonstrates that the Lord took care of unsuspecting people

    c   the young Levite put loyalty ahead of numbers

    d   the names given to Micah's mother, the young Levite, and the five Danites lack distinction

281. **The tragic story of a certain Levite and his concubine had its beginning in the fact that he** [Judges 19:1–30]

    a   never traveled in the heat of the day

    b   accepted overnight accommodations in a strange city

    c   started too early

    d   accepted his father-in-law's invitation to stay overnight

282. **When certain ungodly men of Gibeah demanded that the hospitable old man let them get at his guest, the Levite, he** [Judges 19:22–24]

    a   tried to buy them off with his virgin daughter and the Levite's concubine

    b   fired the house rather than yield

    c   sent to all the people of Israel, from Dan to Beersheba, for aid

    d   meekly gave in to their demand

283. **The seven hundred left-handed Benjamites who could sling stones at an hair breadth and not miss**
[Judges 20:16–48]

    a   were decisive in the first day's battle of the Benjamites with the rest of the Israelites

    b   were decisive in the second day's slaughter of 18,000 Israelites

    c   were deprived of their skill by the shock of the third day's combat

    d   disappear from the story

284. **The tribe of Benjamin was saved from extinction by**
[Judges 21:6–23; 20:47]

    a   four hundred young virgins of Jabesh-gilead and two hundred dancers of Shiloh

  b two hundred young virgins of Jabesh-gilead and
     four hundred dancers of Shiloh
  c the Israelites' abjuration of their oath never to let
     their daughters marry Benjamites
  d their defense of their own women in the cities

Ruth

285. **Ruth was the indirect beneficiary of**   [Ruth 1:1–4]
  a a famine
  b an earthquake
  c a hailstorm
  d a flood

286. **After Naomi's family moved from Bethlehem-judah to
     Moab she lost by death her**   [Ruth 1:3–5]
  a husband
  b husband and one son
  c husband and two sons
  d husband, two sons, and one daughter-in-law

287. **Retracing her steps to the land of Judah ten years later,
     Naomi urged her daughters-in-law to stay in Moab in
     order to**   [Ruth 1:7–13]
  a be sure of enough food
  b obtain husbands
  c avoid rape on the way
  d free herself of quarrelsome daughters-in-law

288. **Naomi and Ruth reached Bethlehem**   [Ruth 1:22]
  a at the beginning of the barley harvest
  b in the middle of the barley harvest
  c just as the barley harvest was ending
  d in the dead of winter

289. **Ruth's plan for finding a husband was to**   [Ruth 2:1–3]
  a stand at the city gate in the presence of the elders
  b help on the threshing floor
  c glean in the field after the reapers
  d lament

290. **Boaz spoke kindly to Ruth because**   [Ruth 2:4–12]
  a the servant in charge of the reapers remarked that
     she had worked without resting
  b he had heard of all that she had done for her mother-
     in-law
  c he was naturally courteous to young women
  d the harvest was good

291. **That Ruth should lie at the feet of Boaz on the threshing floor was the idea of** [Ruth 3:1-4]
    a Boaz
    b Ruth
    c Naomi
    d the city elders

292. **When Boaz found Ruth at his feet he was impressed because she had not followed** [Ruth 3:10]
    a a rich man
    b a young man
    c a transient
    d an elder of the city

293. **Ruth's next of kin would not buy the field Naomi was about to sell, because Ruth went with it, and**
    [Ruth 4:1-6; 3:12-13; 1:1-6]
    a he did not love Ruth
    b Boaz offered him a better field for the same price
    c he would have to restore the name of Mahlon to the property
    d he was married already

294. **When one plucked off his shoe and gave it to another, it signified** [Ruth 4:7]
    a confirmation of a transfer
    b an insult
    c an invitation to dinner
    d an agreement that he would go away

295. **Ruth bore Boaz a son, and Boaz thereby was to become the great grandfather of** [Ruth 4:17]
    a Saul
    b Jesse
    c David
    d Samuel

1 Samuel

296. **Hannah promised the Lord that if He would give her a son she would** [1 Samuel 1:9-11]
    a give him to Peninnah
    b never let a razor come upon his head
    c name him Elkanah
    d make a pilgrimage to Jerusalem

297. **Eli thought Hannah was** [1 Samuel 1:12-14]
    a desolate

b   dissolute
c   drunken
d   delightful

298. **Eli's sons persisted in improprieties, even lying with the women who assembled at the door of the tabernacle, because the Lord**   [1 Samuel 2:22–25]
a   was determined to slay them
b   could make no impress on their minds
c   was indifferent to their fate
d   hoped their excesses would sober them

299. **From Dan to Beersheba all Israel knew that**
[1 Samuel 3:20]
a   Eli's sons, Hophni and Phinehas, would die on the same day
b   the time was coming when there would never be an old man in the house of Eli
c   Samuel was established to be a prophet of the Lord
d   the Lord had called Samuel four times before he realized who was speaking

300. **The fright induced in the Philistines by the Israelites' ark of the covenant caused them to**   [1 Samuel 4:5–11]
a   win the battle
b   lose the battle
c   avoid battle
d   panic

301. **Eli fell and died of a broken neck when he was brought news of**   [1 Samuel 4:16–18]
a   Hophni and Phinehas
b   the ark of God
c   Samuel
d   his daughter-in-law

302. **The Israelites' plea for a king to judge them was not based on**   [1 Samuel 8:1–9]
a   the conduct of Joel and Abiah
b   a desire to be like other nations
c   their rejection of the Lord as their King
d   the stability afforded by the principle of consanguinity

303. **Samuel selected Saul to be captain over the people because**   [1 Samuel 9:15–17]
a   he was impressed by Saul's consideration for his father
b   Saul was of the tribe of Benjamites
c   Saul was willing to consult a seer, to find his lost asses
d   the Lord told him to

304. **Nahash the Ammonite agreed to lift his siege of Jabesh-gilead on the condition that**   [1 Samuel 11:1–2]
a   he thrust out all their right eyes

    b   he cut off their big toes and thumbs
    c   they work twenty hours a day
    d   they renounce Saul

305. **The Israelites made Saul their king** [1 Samuel 11:11–15]
    a   before the battle at Jabesh-gilead
    b   during the battle of Jabesh-gilead
    c   immediately after the battle of Jabesh-gilead
    d   five years after the battle of Jabesh-gilead

306. **The story of Samuel indicates that, as between obedience and burnt offerings, the Lord** [1 Samuel 15:17–28]
    a   preferred obedience
    b   preferred burnt offerings
    c   would as soon have the one as the other
    d   did not commit Himself

307. **When Saul tried to detain Samuel by laying hold upon the skirt of his robe,** [1 Samuel 15:27]
    a   it pulled off
    b   it stuck to Saul's fingers
    c   it tore
    d   nothing happened

308. **While David was refreshing Saul with the harp, the fact that the Lord had chosen David to be his successor was evidently** [1 Samuel 16:1–2, 11–13, 19–23]
    a   not known to Saul
    b   known to Saul but not to David
    c   known to both David and Saul
    d   suspected by Saul

309. **The Lord having admonished Samuel not to look on countenance or height of stature in conjecturing which of Jesse's sons would be chosen king, He selected David, who was** [1 Samuel 16:7, 12]
    a   stumpy, with a game leg
    b   of a beautiful countenance
    c   simply undistinguished looking
    d   aquiline of nose, with heavy brows

310. **In English measure, Goliath's height was** [1 Samuel 17:4]
    a   8 feet 3 inches
    b   9 feet 9 inches
    c   12 feet 3 inches
    d   21 feet 7 inches

311. **The idea of a two-man contest to decide the battle was** [1 Samuel 17:8–10]
    a   Goliath's
    b   David's
    c   Saul's
    d   the Lord's

312. **Goliath presented himself successively for** [1 Samuel 17:16]

    a   seven days
    b   thirteen days
    c   forty days
    d   one hundred days

313. David came into the battle line because
                                [1 Samuel 17:17–22]
    a   he was carrying provisions to his brothers and their commander
    b   the Lord commanded him to do so
    c   his eldest brother Eliab had taunted him
    d   he had heard of the fear inspired by Goliath

314. "For who is this uncircumcised Philistine, that he should defy the armies of the living God?" was uttered by
                                [1 Samuel 17:26]
    a   David
    b   Eliab
    c   Saul
    d   Goliath

315. Eliab's attitude toward David was one of
                                [1 Samuel 17:28]
    a   encouragement
    b   hostility
    c   deprecation
    d   protectiveness

316. David was sure that he could conquer Goliath because of his experience as   [1 Samuel 17:32–37]
    a   a shepherd
    b   a mountain climber
    c   the youngest of eight brothers
    d   a confidant of the Lord

317. David met Goliath without armour because
                                [1 Samuel 17:38–39]
    a   Saul withheld it
    b   no one could be persuaded to surrender his to David
    c   Goliath opined that it would make no difference
    d   David was not used to it

318. David's armory consisted of his sling and smooth stones to the number of   [1 Samuel 17:40]
    a   one
    b   two
    c   four
    d   five

319. Goliath faced David   [1 Samuel 17:41]
    a   alone
    b   with one other man
    c   flanked by two others
    d   at the head of a file of ten

320. **When David had killed Goliath he had left in his wallet, we may infer,** [1 Samuel 17:49–50]

    a no stones
    b two stones
    c three stones
    d four stones

321. **David's best friend's father turned out to be his**
[1 Samuel 18:1–4, 6–11, 29; 14:49]

    a benefactor
    b enemy
    c teacher
    d brother-in-law

322. **The only marriage present Saul asked of David was**
[1 Samuel 18:25]

    a Goliath's head
    b David's lyre
    c a hundred foreskins of the Philistines
    d a hundred Philistine thumbs and a hundred great toes

323. **Saul repeatedly attempted to kill David by**
[1 Samuel 18:11; 19:9–10]

    a poisoning his food
    b pinning him to the wall with a javelin
    c persuading him to be reckless in battle
    d inducing in him suicidal tendencies

324. **David would almost surely have been killed by Saul had it not been for** [1 Samuel 19:1–6, 11–17]

    a Saul's son and daughter
    b David's brothers
    c David's father
    d Samuel

325. **When Saul, like his messengers sent to capture David, took to prophesying when he saw Samuel and the prophets, David** [1 Samuel 19:20–24; 20:1]

    a took the opportunity of imprisoning Saul
    b forgave Saul
    c persuaded Samuel to drive the evil spirit out of Saul
    d fled to Jonathan for help

326. **Saul pointed out to Jonathan that as long as David was alive Jonathan would** [1 Samuel 20:30–31]

    a never be Saul's successor
    b be in danger from David
    c be suspected of improper affection
    d participate in patronage

327. **David feigned madness to escape from**
[1 Samuel 21:12–15]

    a Saul
    b Achish

c   Doeg the Edomite
d   Jonathan

328. **David's repeated successes in escaping from Saul's pursuits were never due to**   [1 Samuel 23:21, 22]
a   warning from the Lord
b   Philistine raids
c   the Prophet Gad
d   paid informers

329. **David passed up the chance to kill Saul in the cave**
                                          [1 Samuel 24:3–6]
a   for the same reason that Hamlet passed up his chance to kill Claudius
b   because Saul had too many followers with him
c   out of sympathy
d   because Saul was the Lord's anointed

330. **David would never have been able to convince Saul that he had spared him, had not David done**
                                          [1 Samuel 24:9–20, 4–6]
a   that for which his heart smote him
b   that which he had planned, just for this argument
c   something in jest
d   more than his men had urged him to do

331. **Nabal's wife Abigail persuaded David not to kill her husband by pointing out that otherwise David would**
                                          [1 Samuel 25:23–33]
a   be pursued anew by Saul
b   have cause of grief and offense of heart
c   be unable to marry her, as widow of the man he murdered
d   be preempting the Lord, who was about to kill Nabal Himself

332. **Including Abigail, the number of wives that David had with him at that time was**   [1 Samuel 25:42–44]
a   one
b   two
c   three
d   four

333. **Saul finally stopped pursuing David when**
                                          [1 Samuel 27:1–4; 26:7–12]
a   David demonstrated the second time (the spear and the cruse of water) that he had had Saul's life in his hands, yet had spared him
b   Jonathan threatened to lead an uprising against his father
c   David's earlier wife, Michal, threatened to denounce publicly her father, Saul
d   David moved his residence to Gath, in the Philistine country

334. **David, in his raids upon the Geshurites, the Gezrites, and the Amalekites, left neither man nor woman alive, in order that** [1 Samuel 27:8–12]
    a these ancient enemies would no more trouble Israel
    b Saul would be impressed by his loyalty to the cause of Israel
    c the Philistine king would never know that it was not Israelites that David was destroying
    d the Lord should be avenged on these worshipers of false gods

335. **After Saul had consulted the woman of Endor that had a familiar spirit, he may well have wished that she had had** [1 Samuel 28:7–20]
    a less power
    b more power
    c no power
    d a more pleasing appearance

336. **The woman of Endor proved** [1 Samuel 28:21–25]
    a vicious
    b hospitable
    c curious
    d dull

337. **David was detached from the Philistine army that was to fight Saul, because** [1 Samuel 29:6–10]
    a he requested it
    b Achish distrusted him
    c the Philistine lords distrusted him
    d of language difficulties

338. **David was enabled to rescue everyone that had been taken from Ziklag, including his two wives, because the Amalekites were** [1 Samuel 30:11–20]
    a cowardly
    b slow
    c undernourished
    d callous

339. **David decreed that those who tarried by the stuff (baggage) would share with those who fought** [1 Samuel 30:21–25]
    a equally
    b as 1 to 2
    c as 1 to 3
    d not at all

340. **At the battle of mount Gilboa, the dead included** [1 Samuel 31:1–6]
    a Jonathan and Saul
    b Jonathan but not Saul
    c Saul but not Jonathan
    d neither Jonathan nor Saul

2 Samuel

341. **"Stand, I pray thee, upon me, and slay me: for anguish is come upon me, because my life is yet whole in me,"** was said by   [2 Samuel 1:8–9]
   a   Saul to an Amalekite
   b   Saul to his armour-bearer
   c   Jonathan to Saul
   d   Saul to Jonathan

342. **"How are the mighty fallen!"** was said of
                           [2 Samuel 1:17, 19, 25]
   a   Saul, by the Amalekite
   b   Saul and Jonathan, by David
   c   David, by Abiathar
   d   David, by Saul

343. **"Tell it not in Gath,"** lest   [2 Samuel 1:20]
   a   the Philistine army rejoice
   b   the Philistine daughters rejoice
   c   the Israelite populace lose heart
   d   Gath be the next attacked

344. **The gathering at the pool of Gibeon ended in**
                           [2 Samuel 2:12–17]
   a   dancing
   b   swimming
   c   oratory
   d   bloodshed

345. **Upon Saul's death**   [2 Samuel 3:1]
   a   the house of Saul fought long with the house of David
   b   all the Israelites rallied to David
   c   all the Israelites forsook David for Abner, of Saul's house
   d   the Israelite kingdom broke into small warring fragments

346. **David's six sons were born**   [2 Samuel 3:2–5]
   a   each of a different woman
   b   two of one wife, four of another
   c   all of one wife
   d   all of one concubine

347. **Ishbosheth, the son of Saul, lost a kingdom because he accused his general, Abner, of**   [2 Samuel 3:6–10]
   a   greed
   b   gluttony

    c   sloth
    d   concupiscence

348. **Abner lost his life owing to others'**   [2 Samuel 3:27, 30]
    a   fatherly caution
    b   soldierly recklessness
    c   brotherly affection
    d   civic pride

349. **David dispensed, to those who brought him news of the death of Saul and the death of Ishbosheth,**
                      [2 Samuel 4:5–12; 1:1–16]
    a   money
    b   praise
    c   imprisonment
    d   death

350. **When David was made king he was**   [2 Samuel 5:4]
    a   twenty
    b   thirty
    c   forty
    d   fifty

351. **When Uzzah put forth his hand to keep the ark of God from falling off the cart when the oxen shook it, the Lord**   [2 Samuel 6:6–7]
    a   decreed that his descendants should flourish
    b   took no notice
    c   warned him not to do it again
    d   killed him

352. **When Michal saw David leaping and dancing before the Lord, girded with a linen ephod, she**
                      [2 Samuel 6:2, 4, 14–23]
    a   approved, to her sorrow
    b   was indifferent
    c   disapproved, to her benefit
    d   disapproved, to her sorrow

353. **In David's bureaucracy, Jehoshaphat was a**
                      [2 Samuel 8:16]
    a   priest
    b   secretary
    c   recorder
    d   treasurer

354. **David asked if anyone was left of the house of Saul; if so, he wanted to**   [2 Samuel 9:1]
    a   send him into exile, to forestall insurrection
    b   show him kindness, for the sake of Jonathan
    c   gather information for a biography of Saul
    d   uncover the truth about the woman of Endor

355. **King David's infatuation with Bathsheba led to her husband's, Uriah the Hittite's,**   [2 Samuel 11:1–17]
    a   promotion

    b   enrichment
    c   banishment
    d   death

356. **The infatuation of King David's son, Amnon, with his sister Tamar, whom he raped, led to his**
                                        [2 Samuel 13:1–29]
    a   promotion
    b   enrichment
    c   banishment
    d   death

357. **Amnon's brother Absalom polled his head**
                                        [2 Samuel 14:26]
    a   once a week
    b   once a month
    c   once a year
    d   never

358. **Absalom stole the hearts of the men of Israel by his**
                                        [2 Samuel 15:2–6]
    a   ingenuity
    b   disingenuousness
    c   ingenuousness
    d   contentiousness

359. **Fleeing from Absalom, King David ordered the ark of God**   [2 Samuel 15:13–14, 24–26]
    a   sent on before him to the Jordan
    b   kept with him as he fled
    c   sent back into Jerusalem
    d   destroyed

360. **When Absalom, in the sight of all Israel, went into a tent on the roof where his father's concubines were, he was, in effect, avenging**   [2 Samuel 16:21–23; 12:9–12]
    a   Ishbosheth
    b   Hanun
    c   Tamar
    d   Uriah

361. **The woman of Bahurim spread ground corn on a covering over a well's mouth to**   [2 Samuel 17:15–21]
    a   speed the sprouting of seed corn by the moisture from below
    b   conceal the well from thirsty wayfarers
    c   trap her neighbor's poultry
    d   hide the messengers to King David from Absalom's servants

362. **When Absalom rejected the counsel of Ahithophel to pursue David with a small force and spare all of David's companions, Ahithophel**   [2 Samuel 17:1–3, 23]
    a   defected to David
    b   loyally obeyed

    c sulked in his house
    d hanged himself

363. **Joab was replaced as commander of the armed forces under Absalom by his** [2 Samuel 17:25]
    a aunt's grandson
    b cousin's husband
    c nephew's father
    d brother

364. **Absalom's mule having carried him under the thick boughs of a great oak so that his head was caught in the oak, Absalom was** [2 Samuel 18:9–15]
    a left hanging from the tree, alive
    b killed immediately because his neck was broken
    c left standing but unable to move
    d slowly strangled

365. **David's cry, "O Absalom," was one of** [2 Samuel 18:33]
    a triumph
    b rebuke
    c recognition
    d grief

366. **After he had helped win the battle in the wood of Ephraim for David, Joab was**
                                        [2 Samuel 19:13; 17:25; 18:6]
    a confirmed for life as commander of David's army
    b retired with honors and rich rewards
    c given David's daughter in marriage
    d replaced by the commander of Absalom's forces, Amasa

367. **The eighty-year-old Barzillai, when King David invited him to stay with him in Jerusalem,** [2 Samuel 19:32–37]
    a jumped for joy
    b backed off suspiciously
    c inquired about the accommodations
    d gracefully declined

368. **Upon his return to Jerusalem, David's ten concubines (see No. 360) were** [2 Samuel 20:3]
    a restored to David's bedchamber
    b executed
    c shut up for the rest of their lives
    d hired out as prostitutes

369. **The head of Sheba, thrown over the wall to Joab, was that of a** [2 Samuel 20:14–22, 1–2]
    a rebel
    b queen
    c priest
    d general

370. **All that the Gibeonites said they wanted as reparation for Saul's attempts to destroy them was seven**
      [2 Samuel 21:3–6]

      a   cities of Israel to occupy
      b   concubines of David to prostitute
      c   men of the sons of Saul to hang
      d   years of peace

371. **In his encounter with a descendant of the giants, one whose spear weighed 300 shekels of brass, David**
      [2 Samuel 21:15–17]

      a   won, again with a slingshot
      b   won, but with a sword
      c   was rescued by Abishai
      d   ran away

372. **The song of David to the Lord gave Him thanks chiefly for**   [2 Samuel 22:1–51; 23:1–7]

      a   strength to resist temptation
      b   growth of the population of Israel
      c   a long life
      d   military victories

373. **When the Lord gave David his choice of three punishments, David expressed an explicit preference for**
      [2 Samuel 24:11–15]

      a   seven years of famine
      b   three months of flight
      c   three days of pestilence
      d   no one of these three

1 Kings

374. **His servants succeeded in keeping the old King David warm by**   [1 Kings 1:1–3]
      a   covering him with clothes
      b   bringing a fair virgin to lie with him
      c   exciting him with news of Adonijah
      d   crowding his room with people

375. **The second of King David's sons that tried to oust him from the throne, Adonijah, was born**   [1 Kings 1:5–6]
      a   the last before Absalom
      b   at the same time as Absalom
      c   after Absalom
      d   no one knows when

376. **The initiative to persuade King David to oppose his son Adonijah in favor of his son Solomon was taken by**
[1 Kings 1:11–14]
   a   Nathan the prophet
   b   Bathsheba
   c   Joab
   d   Ahinoam

377. **The successor to King David was the son of**
[1 Kings 1:39; 2 Samuel 11:3, 17; 12:24]
   a   Haggith
   b   the widow of Nabal
   c   the widow of Uriah
   d   Abishag

378. **Upon gaining the throne, Solomon dealt with Adonijah by immediately**   [1 Kings 1:50–53]
   a   killing him
   b   exiling him
   c   pardoning him
   d   sending him to his own house

379. **Adonijah's request to Bathsheba to gain Solomon's consent to his marrying the maiden who had warmed the old King David reflected**   [1 Kings 2:13–25]
   a   generosity
   b   statesmanship
   c   quick thinking
   d   poor judgment

380. **When King Solomon married the daughter of the ruler of the country that had oppressed the Israelites, the Lord expressed**   [1 Kings 3:1]
   a   fury
   b   pleasure
   c   indifference
   d   no opinion

381. **When the Lord said to Solomon, "Ask what I shall give thee," Solomon asked for**   [1 Kings 3:5–9]
   a   an understanding heart
   b   riches
   c   long life
   d   death to his enemies

382. **When King Solomon ordered the disputed child to be cut in half for the two harlots, he counted on mother love to prefer**   [1 Kings 3:16–27]
   a   loss of child to loss of child's life
   b   loss of child's life to loss of child
   c   vengeance on the false claimant
   d   possession of the dead to loss of the living

383. **Solomon spake**   [1 Kings 4:32]
   a   30 proverbs and 15 songs

b 300 proverbs and 105 songs
c 3,000 proverbs and 1,005 songs
d 30,000 proverbs and 10,500 songs

384. **The cedars of Lebanon were**   [1 Kings 5:5–10]
a preserved as a place of worship
b destroyed by fire
c felled to build the house of the Lord
d sanctified as a burial ground

385. **Solomon's own house, in comparison with the house of the Lord he built, was**   [1 Kings 7:1–2; 6:2]
a shorter, narrower, and lower
b longer, narrower, and higher
c shorter, broader, and the same height
d longer, broader, and the same height

386. **The two pillars of brass that Hiram of Tyre cast for King Solomon were in height**   [1 Kings 7:13–15]
a five feet
b twelve feet
c twenty-seven feet
d forty-two feet

387. **The length given for the circumference of King Solomon's molten sea, compared with the diameter given for that same sea, is that to be expected from the geometrical relation, $2\pi r$,**   [1 Kings 7:23]
a exactly
b almost exactly
c not at all, the circumference being far too short
d not at all, the circumference being far too long

388. **The main theme of King Solomon's appeal to the Lord upon dedication of the new house of the Lord was**
[1 Kings 8:22–53]
a destruction of Israel's enemies
b a long reign for King Solomon
c a stay of punishment if Israel erred
d forgiveness of repentant sinners

389. **At that dedication Solomon gave as peace offerings to the Lord**   [1 Kings 8:63]
a 22 oxen and 120 sheep
b 220 oxen and 1,200 sheep
c 2,200 oxen and 12,000 sheep
d 22,000 oxen and 120,000 sheep

390. **"Cabul" refers to**   [1 Kings 9:10–14]
a the houses for which Hiram had supplied the cedar and fir trees and gold
b the planers who designed the houses
c Solomon's wives
d the region containing the twenty cities Solomon gave to Hiram

391. **Pharaoh, King of Egypt, gave his daughter (Solomon's wife) as a present** [1 Kings 9:16]
    a four hundred and twenty talents of gold
    b a crypt in the Great Pyramid
    c a burned and slaughtered city
    d a tapestried houseboat on the River Nile

392. **When the Queen of Sheba visited King Solomon**
                              [1 Kings 10:1–9]
    a she was overawed by him
    b he was overawed by her
    c she became infatuated with him
    d he became infatuated with her

393. **King Solomon possessed** [1 Kings 10:26]
    a 140 chariots
    b 1,400 chariots
    c 14,000 chariots
    d 140,000 chariots

394. **For the same amount of money needed to import a chariot from Egypt in King Solomon's time, one could import** [1 Kings 10:29]
    a half a horse
    b one horse
    c four horses
    d twenty horses

395. **King Solomon had** [1 Kings 11:3]
    a 7 wives and 3 concubines
    b 70 wives and 30 concubines
    c 700 wives and 300 concubines
    d 7,000 wives and 3,000 concubines

396. **Milcom was a** [1 Kings 11:33]
    a god
    b river
    c sedative
    d disease

397. **Solomon reigned over all Israel** [1 Kings 11:42; 2:11]
    a forty years, as had David
    b forty years, unlike David
    c less than forty years, like David
    d more than forty years, unlike David

398. **Rehoboam, the son of Solomon who succeeded to his throne, said, "My father also chastised you with whips, but I will chastise you with scorpions," in addressing the** [1 Kings 11:43; 12:3–4, 13–14]
    a Israelites
    b Amorites
    c Hittites
    d Jebusites

399. **The Lord allowed Rehoboam to retain control over only a small portion of all Israel, because of**
                            [1 Kings 12:17-20; 11:4-13]
   a   his harshness
   b   Solomon's apostasy
   c   David's killings
   d   Saul's suicide

400. **Jeroboam, reigning over all the other tribes of Israel, forbade them to go to the house of the Lord in Jerusalem, because**   [1 Kings 12:19-20, 26-28]
   a   he himself believed in the golden calf
   b   he feared they would turn again to Rehoboam
   c   he believed Rehoboam had set ambushes for them
   d   the Lord had instructed him to do so

401. **Sodomites were a feature of**   [1 Kings 14:21-24]
   a   Judah, under Rehoboam
   b   the rest of Israel, under Jeroboam
   c   the tribe of Levites
   d   the prophets of Bethel

402. **Jehu the prophet brought**   [1 Kings 16:1-4, 12-13]
   a   good news
   b   bad news
   c   unintelligible news
   d   no news at all

403. **Jezebel was**   [1 Kings 16:29-31]
   a   the wife of a wicked Israelite king
   b   the deceitful concubine of a good Israelite king
   c   a god of the Ammonites
   d   a town in Judah

404. **The ravens brought Elijah**   [1 Kings 17:1, 6]
   a   water
   b   flesh and oil
   c   bread and flesh
   d   nothing at all

405. **The widow's cruse was kept miraculously full of**
                            [1 Kings 17:10-16]
   a   oil
   b   water
   c   bread
   d   flesh

406. **The widow Elijah befriended became convinced that he was a man of God when**   [1 Kings 17:17-24]
   a   her son was revived
   b   the barrel wasted not
   c   the cruse did not fail
   d   the ravens came

407. **Obadiah, who had been brave enough to hide one hundred of them when Jezebel was slaying the prophets of**

the Lord, was nevertheless afraid to tell the wicked King
Ahab that Elijah had come, for he feared that

[1 Kings 18:7–14]

a   Ahab would slay Elijah
b   Jezebel would seduce Elijah
c   Jezebel would slay Ahab
d   Elijah would disappear

408. **Jezebel's table accommodated, of the prophets of Baal
and those of the groves, respectively,**   [1 Kings 18:19]
a   45 and 40
b   450 and 400
c   4,500 and 4,000
d   45,000 and 40,000

409. **In Elijah's contest at mount Carmel with the prophets
of Baal for the allegiance of the Israelites,**

[1 Kings 18:22–40]

a   he set the test
b   they set the test
c   the Lord set the test
d   an impartial bystander set the test

410. **The pregnant phrase, "a little cloud out of the sea, like
a man's hand," was uttered by**   [1 Kings 18:42–44]
a   Elijah
b   Elijah's servant
c   Ahab
d   Ahab's servant

411. **"A still small voice" came to Elijah**   [1 Kings 19:11–13]
a   with the cake baked on the coals and the cruse of
    water
b   right after the wind
c   right after the earthquake
d   right after the fire

412. **The Lord decided to leave alive in Israel anyone whose
knees had not bowed to Baal and whose mouth had not
kissed him; namely,**   [1 Kings 19:18]
a   70 Israelites
b   700 Israelites
c   7,000 Israelites
d   70,000 Israelites

413. **Ben-hadad, King of Syria, came to grief because of**

[1 Kings 20:1–21]

a   greed
b   modesty
c   indecisiveness
d   inefficiency

414. **Naboth's vineyard proved to be, for him**

[1 Kings 21:1–13]

a   profitable

b   health giving
c   sickening
d   fatal

415. **Jezebel was doomed by the Lord to become**
                                              [1 Kings 21:23]
    a   a ghost
    b   a wandering Jewess
    c   crippled for life
    d   food for dogs

416. **King Ahab's instructions to King Jehoshaphat to go into battle undisguised while he went into it disguised were aimed at**   [1 Kings 22:29–33]
    a   sparing Jehoshaphat's life
    b   sparing his own life
    c   allowing the credit for victory to go to Jehoshaphat
    d   assuring that the blame for defeat rested on Jehoshaphat

2 Kings

417. **King Ahaziah died of his sickness because he**
                                              [2 Kings 1:2–17]
    a   would take no medicine
    b   sought a prognosis from the wrong source
    c   was unaware that he was ill
    d   followed the regime recommended by Baal-zebub

418. **Elijah did not have to obey King Ahaziah's summons to appear before him because he could**   [2 Kings 1:9–12]
    a   outrun the captain and the fifty men sent to fetch him
    b   part the waters of a river with his mantle
    c   open fissures in the earth too wide to cross
    d   call down consuming fire from heaven

419. **Elisha was to inherit a double portion of Elijah's spirit if Elisha**   [2 Kings 2:9–12]
    a   would not search for him after he had been taken from him by the chariot and horses of fire
    b   saw him being taken from him
    c   did not see him being taken from him
    d   would not use Elijah's mantle to part the waters of a river

420. **Elisha's antipollution agent for water was**
                                                  [2 Kings 2:19-22]

    a   salt
    b   pepper
    c   iron
    d   sandalwood

421. **When some little children came out of Bethel and mocked Elisha, he**   [2 Kings 2:23-24]

    a   paid no attention
    b   inquired into their family backgrounds
    c   had them apprehended
    d   cursed them in the name of the Lord so that she bears tore forty-two of them

422. **Elisha's power of prophecy was stirred by a**
                                                  [2 Kings 3:15]

    a   dancer
    b   minstrel
    c   wind
    d   priest

423. **When the Moabites saw the water opposite them as red as blood, they**   [2 Kings 3:22-23]

    a   fled from the Israelites in fear
    b   attacked the Israelites with optimism
    c   fought one another in panic
    d   were rooted to the ground with astonishment

424. **The victorious Israelites ruined the Moabites' lands by**
                                                  [2 Kings 3:25]

    a   sowing them with salt
    b   covering them with stones
    c   criss-crossing them with ditches
    d   carrying away the topsoil

425. **Through Elisha's intervention, the widow filled with oil several**   [2 Kings 4:1-7]

    a   vessels
    b   jars
    c   buckets
    d   cruses

426. **Elisha did not**   [2 Kings 4:39-44; 5:1-14, 20-27]

    a   neutralize the pottage poison by casting meal into the pot
    b   cause twenty loaves of barley and full ears of corn to suffice for 100 men
    c   cure the Syrian army commander of leprosy
    d   cure his servant of leprosy

427. **The Syrians stopped their raids into Israel after Elisha had caused the Syrian army to be blinded and had**
                                                  [2 Kings 6:8, 18-23]

    a   sold them into captivity

    b   restored their sight and sent them home
    c   kept them as servants
    d   let them beg through Israel

428. **The woman in the siege of Samaria who had boiled her son and eaten him with another woman begged the king for help because**   [2 Kings 6:26–29]
    a   the second woman had hidden her son
    b   her conscience was tormenting her to insanity
    c   she was still frantic with hunger
    d   she sought death but dared not achieve it

429. **The question, "If the Lord would make windows in heaven, might this thing be?" proved to be, for the speaker,**   [2 Kings 7:2, 17]
    a   fortunate
    b   farseeing
    c   fatal
    d   fortuitous

430. **The Syrians panicked and so lifted the siege, under an illusion of**   [2 Kings 7:6–7]
    a   sight
    b   hearing
    c   touch
    d   smell

431. **The number of camel loads of goods that Ben-hadad sent to Elisha as a present was**   [2 Kings 8:7–9]
    a   seven
    b   thirteen
    c   forty
    d   seventy-seven

432. **When Hazael smothered his ailing King Ben-hadad with a wet cloth, he was merely doing**   [2 Kings 8:7–15]
    a   what ambitious men in Syria had done before
    b   nothing inconsistent with what he had heard Elisha prophesy
    c   what Elisha had commanded him to do
    d   what the ill king had begged him to do

433. **To drive like Jehu means to drive**   [2 Kings 9:20]
    a   cautiously
    b   skillfully
    c   awkwardly
    d   furiously

434. **Jehu, newly anointed king of Israel, himself killed with bow and arrow**   [2 Kings 9:3, 6, 24, 27]
    a   King Jehoram of Israel
    b   King Ahaziah of Judah
    c   both King Jehoram and King Ahaziah
    d   neither King Jehoram nor King Ahaziah

435. **Jezebel painted her face and tired her head shortly before**   [2 Kings 9:30–37]
   a   seducing Jehu
   b   burying Jehoram
   c   being killed
   d   going into exile

436. **Overawed by Jehu, Samaria sent him seventy**
                                              [2 Kings 10:1–8]
   a   talents of gold
   b   heads of men
   c   renegade priests
   d   prophets of Baal

437. **Jehu made the house of Baal a**   [2 Kings 10:27]
   a   draught house
   b   monument
   c   hostel
   d   refuge

438. **Athaliah, mother of King Ahaziah, tried to slay her**
                                              [2 Kings 11:1–3]
   a   husband
   b   sons
   c   grandsons
   d   brothers

439. **Athaliah was killed at the order of**   [2 Kings 11:13–16]
   a   her husband
   b   one of her sons
   c   the priest of one of her grandsons
   d   one of her brothers

440. **Athaliah's grandson Joash was killed by his**
                                              [2 Kings 12:20]
   a   grandmother
   b   brother
   c   son
   d   servants

441. **The lesson that Joash learned from Elisha's command to smite the ground with the arrows was**
                                              [2 Kings 13:14–19]
   a   enough is enough
   b   finish the job
   c   easy does it
   d   an ounce of caution outweighs a pound of valor

442. **Azariah, King of Judah, stricken with leprosy because the Lord was angry with him,**   [2 Kings 15:1–5]
   a   dwelt in a separate house
   b   lived as would a king without leprosy
   c   was exiled to a leper colony
   d   was stoned to death

443. **Taking the thirteen successive kings of Judah, from Rehoboam to Ahaz, and the contemporaneous eighteen kings of Israel, from Jeroboam to Hoshea, we find that the kings that were slain by their successors were**
[From 1 Kings 14:20 to 2 Kings 16:20 *passim*]
a none in Judah and seven in Israel
b two in Judah and five in Israel
c four in Judah and three in Israel
d seven in Judah and none in Israel

444. **The line of kings of Israel ended with Hoshea as in his reign all the remaining people of Israel were carried away into**   [2 Kings 17:3, 6, 23]
a Egypt, by King So
b Assyria, by King Sennacherib
c Babylon, by King Tiglath-pileser
d Assyria, by King Shalmaneser

445. **"I will put my hook in thy nose, and my bridle in thy lips," said the Lord, referring to**
[2 Kings 19:20–21, 28, 32]
a Isaiah
b Hoshea
c Sennacherib
d Shalmaneser

446. **The angel of the Lord came to the rescue of Hezekiah and "the remnant that is escaped of the house of Judah" in Jerusalem by killing, in one night,**
[2 Kings 19:30, 35]
a 1,850 Assyrians
b 18,500 Assyrians
c 185,000 Assyrians
d 1,850,000 Assyrians

447. **Hezekiah received the Lord's message, that his wealth would some day be carried to Babylon and that his sons would be eunuchs there, with**   [2 Kings 20:16–19]
a complacency
b disbelief
c sorrow
d horror

448. **"I will wipe Jerusalem as a man wipeth a dish, wiping it, and turning it upside down," said**   [2 Kings 21:12–13]
a the Lord
b Sennacherib
c Manasseh
d Hephzibah

449. **King Josiah was motivated to the wholesale destruction of idols and their groves and altars, and the removal of idolatrous priests, workers with familiar spirits, and wizards by what he found in a**
[2 Kings 22:11–13; 23:1–24]

    a   book
    b   brook
    c   dream
    d   tomb

450. **The Lord, weighing the good deeds of King Josiah, who "turned to the Lord with all his heart, and with all his soul, and with all his might," against the evil deeds of his grandfather, King Manasseh, apparently concluded that the**   [2 Kings 23:25–27]
    a   good outweighed the evil
    b   evil outweighed the good
    c   two were equally balanced
    d   two could not be compared

451. **King Josiah's son, King Eliakim, was forced to adopt another name, by**   [2 Kings 23:34]
    a   King Nebuchadnezzar
    b   Pharaoh-nechoh
    c   his mother, Zebudah
    d   the Lord

452. **The King Zedekiah, Jehoiachin's uncle, who rebelled against Nebuchadnezzar and lost, was punished by**
          [2 Kings 24:17, 20; 25:1–7]
    a   having his sons put to death before his eyes
    b   being blinded and taken in fetters to Babylon
    c   both a and b
    d   neither a nor b

453. **The story of the destruction of Jerusalem and the captivity or dispersion of the people of Judah ends with the new Babylonian king, Evil-merodach,**
          [2 Kings 25:27–30]
    a   slaying the imprisoned Jehoiachin
    b   slaying the imprisoned Zedekiah
    c   freeing Jehoiachin
    d   freeing Zedekiah

1 Chronicles

454. **The Philistines were descendants of**
          [1 Chronicles 1:4, 8, 11, 12]
    a   Shem
    b   Ham
    c   Japheth
    d   neither Shem, Ham, nor Japheth

455. **The mother of Jabez gave him that name because**
[1 Chronicles 4:9]
   a   he was a surprise
   b   the Lord told her to
   c   she bore him in sorrow
   d   there was a famine in the land

456. **Elhanan slew Goliath's**
[1 Chronicles 20:5; 2 Samuel 21:19]
   a   brother
   b   sister
   c   uncle
   d   nephew

457. **David was forbidden by the Lord to build the house of rest for the ark of the covenant, because the Lord**
[1 Chronicles 28:2–3]
   a   considered him a poor architect
   b   thought the Israelites did not yet deserve it
   c   decided that the ark should never be put inside a house
   d   deplored David's warrior habits

458. **The pattern of the porch of the house for the sanctuary, and of its treasuries, chambers, parlors, and the like, were**   [1 Chronicles 28:11–12]
   a   given by David to his son Solomon
   b   submitted by Solomon for David's approval
   c   drawn up by Solomon without asking David's approval
   d   revealed to Solomon by the Lord

2 Chronicles

459. **In 2 Chronicles 2 it tells us what 1 Kings 5 did not, that the 70,000 bearers of burdens, the 80,000 hewers in the mountain, and the 3,600 (3,300 in 1 Kings 5) overseers engaged in Solomon's huge building program were**
[2 Chronicles 2:17–18; 1 Kings 5:15–16]
   a   volunteer Israelites
   b   impressed Israelites
   c   strangers attracted to Israel by this public works project
   d   impressed strangers resident in Israel

460. **Solomon brought his wife, Pharaoh's daughter, up from Jerusalem to the house he had built for her because** [2 Chronicles 8:11]
   a she did not like Jerusalem's climate
   b no house in Jerusalem was big enough for her
   c Jerusalem was too far from Egypt
   d the house of David was holy

461. **"My little finger shall be thicker than my father's loins," is what** [2 Chronicles 10:10; see 1 Kings 12:10]
   a Solomon said to the Hittites
   b Rehoboam said to Solomon
   c Rehoboam's young advisers said Rehoboam should say to the Israelites
   d Solomon's old advisers said Rehoboam should say to the Hittites

462. **When, after Solomon, the Israelites split into those under Jeroboam and those (of Judah and Benjamin) under Rehoboam, all of the priestly tribe, the Levites, came to Rehoboam because** [2 Chronicles 11:1, 13–17]
   a they wanted to officiate in Jerusalem
   b Jeroboam had cast them off from serving as priests
   c Rehoboam offered them more perquisites
   d the Lord told them to

463. **King Rehoboam had, per wife and concubine,**
                                    [2 Chronicles 11:21]
   a 1.13 children
   b 1.78 children
   c 2.71 children
   d 4.16 children

464. **Shishak was** [2 Chronicles 12:2; see 1 Kings 14:25]
   a the birthplace of Rehoboam
   b the king of Egypt
   c a Lebanese dish of roast lamb
   d the fourth most sacred day in the Israelite calendar

465. **When King Abijah, with 400,000 men, fought King Jeroboam, with 800,000 men,** [2 Chronicles 13:3, 17]
   a Abijah lost 150,000 men
   b Jeroboam lost 350,000 men
   c Abijah lost 250,000 men
   d Jeroboam lost 500,000 men

466. **King Abijah, Rehoboam's son, had, per wife (no concubines mentioned),** [2 Chronicles 13:21]
   a 1.13 children
   b 1.78 children
   c 2.71 children
   d 4.16 children

467. **King Asa's army of 580,000 men from Judah and Benjamin defeated an Ethiopian army of**
                                    [2 Chronicles 14:8–9, 12–13]

    a   200,000 men
    b   500,000 men
    c   800,000 men
    d 1,000,000 men

468. **King Asa, whose heart was perfect all his days, nevertheless committed one grave error: when Baasha, King of Israel, warred against him, Asa**
[2 Chronicles 15:17; 16:1-3, 7-9]
    a decided not to ask help from the King of Syria
    b asked help from the King of Syria instead of from the Lord
    c declared war on the King of Syria
    d never considered the King of Syria

469. **In the wilderness of Tekoa, Jehoshaphat's forces were victorious over the men of Ammon, Moab, and mount Seir**   [2 Chronicles 20:20, 22-23]
    a without raising a hand themselves
    b by setting an ambush with the aid of the Lord
    c at the cost of losing half their men
    d by persuasion

470. **King Jehoshaphat, having given the kingdom to his son Jehoram, left to his other sons great gifts of silver, gold, and precious things, together with fenced cities in Judah, but**   [2 Chronicles 21:1-4]
    a to no avail
    b with a guilty conscience
    c under duress
    d with misgivings

471. **Because of his wickedness, King Jehoram was told in a writing from Elijah that he would die from**
[2 Chronicles 21:12-15, 18-19]
    a leprosy
    b his diseased bowels falling out
    c thirst
    d headaches that would crack his skull

472. **Jehoiada, the priest, who put the seven-year-old King Joash on the throne of Judah, was the husband of a daughter of a**   [2 Chronicles 22:1, 11; 23:1, 9-11; 21:1]
    a king of Israel
    b king of Judah
    c Levite
    d Philistine

473. **After Jehoiada's death, King Joash of Judah had Jehoiada's son Zechariah**   [2 Chronicles 24:17, 20-22]
    a honored
    b ostracized
    c exiled
    d killed

474. **When on command from the Lord, King Amaziah (son**

of Joash of Judah) sent the Israelite mercenaries back
home even after he had paid for them, he averted a
disaster at the cost of   [2 Chronicles 25:6–13]

a loss of face
b monetary loss
c monetary loss and slight property damage
d monetary loss, heavy property damage, and lives

475. **The equipment of Uzziah's army included**
                                              [2 Chronicles 26:14]

a helmets but no coats of mail
b coats of mail and slings to cast stones
c spears but no slings to cast stones
d spears but no army shields

476. **When King Uzziah entered the temple of the Lord to
burn incense on the altar, his priests were**
                                           [2 Chronicles 26:16–18]

a overjoyed
b complacent
c indifferent
d outraged

477. **When King Ahaz, grandson of Uzziah, burned his children as an offering, he was following the practice of**
                              [2 Chronicles 28:1–3; 26:23; 27:9]

a Uzziah
b the worshipers of Baalim
c the Assyrians
d no one in particular

478. **The 200,000 women, sons, and daughters of the men of
Judah taken captive by the men of Israel under King
Pekah were**   [2 Chronicles 28:6–15]

a slaughtered
b made bondmen and bondwomen
c exiled
d sent back home

479. **In 2 Chronicles 28 the name of the King of Assyria is
spelled**   [2 Chronicles 28:20]

a Tiglath-pileser
b Tilgath-pilneser
c Tiglath-pilneser
d Tilgath-pileser

480. **King Hezekiah, son of King Ahaz, decided that the house
of the Lord should be** [2 Chronicles 29:1, 5, 16–19; 28:27]

a cleansed
b sanctified
c cleansed and sanctified
d defiled

481. **King Hezekiah's posts went throughout all Israel and
Judah, with letters inviting the people to come to Jerusalem to**   [2 Chronicles 30:1–6]

  a keep the passover
  b mass against Assyria
  c worship the Baals
  d stimulate tourism

482. **On the whole, Hezekiah's project (on which he sent the posts) must be accounted a**   [2 Chronicles 30:10–27]
  a success
  b failure
  c disaster
  d venture of uncertain value

483. **The heaps of corn, wine, oil, honey, and other things piled up for seven months at King Hezekiah's command were to**   [2 Chronicles 31:4–10]
  a provision the army
  b ward off famine
  c supply the King's household
  d feed the priests and the Levites

484. **Hezekiah stopped all the fountains and the brook that ran through Judah, in order to**   [2 Chronicles 32:2–4]
  a inhibit the worship of water gods
  b discommode Sennacherib
  c raise the water table
  d punish those who did not respond to his couriers

485. **After the commanders of the army of the King of Assyria had taken the evil King Manasseh among the thorns, and bound him with fetters and carried him to Babylon, the Lord**   [2 Chronicles 33:10–13]
  a gave Manasseh another chance to reign in Jerusalem
  b allowed Manasseh to perish in Babylon
  c inspired Manasseh to convert the Assyrians
  d forgot Manasseh

486. **The long exile of the Israelites in Babylon was ended by**
                            [2 Chronicles 36:22–23]
  a Jeremiah, the prophet
  b Cyrus, King of Persia
  c Nebuchadnezzar, King of Babylon
  d Zedekiah, King of Judah

Ezra

487. **The whole congregation that went to rebuild the house of the Lord in Jerusalem numbered, in addition to their servants and their maids and singers,**   [Ezra 1:5; 2:64, 65]

a   423,600
b   42,360
c   4,236
d   424

488. **King Artaxerxes was persuaded to decree that the rebuilding of Jerusalem be halted because of the prospect
that if the city were rebuilt**   [Ezra 4:8, 13, 16–22]
a   too many tourists from Persia would visit it
b   it would stand empty
c   costly infrastructure would be required
d   the Persian revenues would decrease

489. **The rebuilding of Jerusalem had been fostered by King
Darius of Persia because Darius**   [Ezra 5:17; 6:1–12]
a   was opposed to everything that Artaxerxes had stood
for
b   was in favor of promoting tourism to the outer
reaches of the Persian empire
c   had the records searched and found that Cyrus had
indeed initiated this project
d   felt that he owed something to Jerusalem

490. **The journey of Ezra, the scribe skilled in the law of
Moses, from Babylon to Jerusalem took** [Ezra 7:6, 8–9]
a   four days
b   four weeks
c   forty days
d   four months

491. **King Artaxerxes gave Ezra**   [Ezra 7:12–24]
a   a good deal of trouble
b   no help
c   some small assistance
d   lavish aid

492. **Sherebiah, Hashabiah, and Jeshaiah were** [Ezra 8:15–19]
a   Levites sent to Ezra by Iddo
b   Levites sent by Ezra to Iddo
c   non-Levites selected to serve Ezra as priests
d   three old men who guarded Ezra

493. **Ezra says he rent his garment and his mantle, plucked
off the hair of his head and beard, and sat down astonied,
because**   [Ezra 9:1–3]
a   the Persian officials failed to keep their word
b   Sherebiah, Hashabiah and Jeshaiah succumbed to the
Baalim
c   the Lord expressed displeasure at the pace of rebuilding
d   the men of Israel were marrying women of the
Canaanites, Hittites, Perizzites, Jebusites, Ammonites,
Moabites, Egyptians, and Amorites

494. **In the end Ezra**   [Ezra 10:1–17]
    a   succeeded
    b   failed
    c   succeeded somewhat, failed somewhat
    d   ceased to strive

Nehemiah

495. **Nehemiah was**   [Nehemiah 1:1, 11; 2:1]
    a   Ezra's son-in-law
    b   Jehohanan's secretary
    c   King Artaxerxes' cupbearer
    d   Iddo's scribe

496. **Nehemiah secretly inspected the gates and walls of Jerusalem in order to**   [Nehemiah 2:11–16]
    a   find a way of entry for the Israelites
    b   rescue the holy objects immured therein
    c   ascertain the damage they had suffered
    d   compare them with those of Jericho

497. **None of the gates to Jerusalem that Nehemiah mentions bore the name of**   [Nehemiah 2:12–15; 3:1–32]
    a   West Gate
    b   Fish Gate
    c   Old Gate
    d   Dung Gate

498. **Nehemiah's rebuilding progressed rather inefficiently because of**   [Nehemiah 4:16–18]
    a   high interest rates
    b   bad weather
    c   defense measures
    d   lack of planning

499. **Nehemiah had the wall around Jerusalem completed in**
                                         [Nehemiah 6:15]
    a   seven days
    b   forty days
    c   fifty-two days
    d   two hundred and three days

500. **Nehemiah found that Jerusalem was somewhat difficult to defend, because the people within it were**
                                         [Nehemiah 7:3–4]
    a   few
    b   many

    c   unfit
    d   indifferent

501. **In the 87 names given in Nehemiah 10:1–26 in listing the priests, Levites and chiefs (and occasionally their fathers) the most common initial letter is**   [Nehemiah 10:1–26]
    a   A
    b   H
    c   M
    d   V

502. **To prevent transport and sale of goods on the Sabbath in Jerusalem, Nehemiah ordered that**   [Nehemiah 13:15–19]
    a   an extra tithe be imposed
    b   all asses be impounded
    c   the gates be shut
    d   prayer be continuous

Esther

503. **Queen Vashti was demoted for disobedience chiefly because the king feared that**   [Esther 1:10–12, 17–20]
    a   once disobedient, always so
    b   all wives in the kingdom would follow her example
    c   all wives would scorn her because she had disobeyed
    d   foreign potentates would issue no invitations to a husband disobeyed

504. **Before going in to the king, Esther, like all the other beautiful young virgins brought to the court, purified herself with oil of myrrh, sweet odours, and the like for a period of twelve**   [Esther 2:12, 16–17]
    a   minutes
    b   days
    c   weeks
    d   months

505. **Haman persuaded the king to let him order destruction of "a certain people" within the kingdom, having been angered when obeisance was not rendered by Mordecai, Esther's**   [Esther 3:1–15; 2:7]
    a   cousin
    b   nephew
    c   brother
    d   uncle

506. **The king's willingness to grant Haman's request can be reconciled with his love for his Queen Esther by the fact that he**   [Esther 3:7–15; 2:10, 20]
    a did not know that Esther was a Jewess
    b knew she was a Jewess but did not know that Haman's projected victims were Jews
    c thought that Esther was indifferent to the fate of her people
    d was stupid

507. **Esther was reluctant to ask the king to countermand the order because**   [Esther 4:8–11]
    a she recalled what had happened to Vashti
    b the usual penalty for going to the king without being asked was death
    c she feared the vengeance of Haman
    d she could not believe such an order had been issued

508. **Haman had to do honor to the man he sought to hang, as an indirect consequence of the king's**   [Esther 6:1–11]
    a insomnia
    b nightmares
    c dreamless sleep
    d snoring

509. **Haman's final tactical error was, in the presence of the king, to**   [Esther 7:7–8]
    a threaten Esther with bodily harm
    b vilify Esther
    c agree to compulsory arbitration
    d beg his life from Esther

510. **The days of Purim decreed by Queen Esther were so named from**   [Esther 9:24–26]
    a purity
    b poverty
    c gallows
    d the lot

Job

511. **Job was an inhabitant of the land of**   [Job 1:1]
    a Uz
    b Oz
    c Iz
    d Ez

512.   **And he was**   [Job 1:2–3]
       a   poor, but had many children
       b   poor, with no children
       c   rich, with many children
       d   rich, with no children

513.   **The conversation about Job, between the Lord and Satan,
       was initiated by**   [Job 1:6–8]
       a   Satan
       b   the Lord
       c   the Lord and Satan simultaneously
       d   neither the Lord nor Satan

514.   **Job's misfortunes can be traced to the fact that he was
       considered**   [Job 1:9–12]
       a   weak, by both the Lord and Satan
       b   strong, by both the Lord and Satan
       c   weak by the Lord, strong by Satan
       d   strong by the Lord, weak by Satan

515.   **All of Job's children were killed simultaneously in**
                                                          [Job 1:18–19]
       a   an earthquake
       b   a flood
       c   a wind
       d   an epidemic

516.   **"The Lord gave, and the Lord hath taken away," said**
                                                          [Job 1:20–21]
       a   Job
       b   Job's wife
       c   Satan
       d   the Lord

517.   **The reason why Satan did not take Job's wife from him
       is**   [Job 1:1–22; 2:1–10]
       a   that she herself was an affliction
       b   that Satan never attacked women
       c   that Satan overlooked this possibility
       d   not stated

518.   **The sore boils that afflicted Job from the sole of his foot
       unto his crown were the idea of**   [Job 2:4–7]
       a   Satan
       b   the Lord
       c   Job's wife
       d   Job's neighbor

519.   **After seven days and nights of silence with his three
       friends, Job opened his mouth and**   [Job 2:11, 13; 3:1]
       a   praised the Lord
       b   thanked his friends
       c   cursed Satan
       d   cursed his day

520. **The attitude toward Job, of his friend Eliphaz the Te-
manite, was one of**   [Job 4:1–21; 5:1–27]
   a sympathy
   b indifference
   c indulgence
   d reproof

521. **"Yet man is born unto trouble, as the sparks fly upward," said**   [Job 5:7]
   a Job
   b Job's wife
   c Job's friend
   d Satan

522. **"Doth the wild ass bray when he hath grass? or loweth
the ox over his fodder?" asked**   [Job 6:1, 5]
   a Job
   b Eliphaz
   c Bildad
   d Zophar

523. **Job appeared to receive Eliphaz's words with**
                                    [Job 6:14–30; 7:11–21]
   a gratitude
   b hope
   c incredulity
   d reproach

524. **"For we are but of yesterday, and know nothing, because our days upon earth are a shadow," said**
                                           [Job 8:1, 9]
   a Job
   b Eliphaz
   c Bildad
   d Zophar

525. **Job's friend Bildad the Shuhite, on the whole,**
                                           [Job 8:1–22]
   a agreed with Eliphaz
   b disagreed with Eliphaz
   c refrained from comment
   d agreed with Job

526. **In response, Job evidenced**   [Job 9; 10]
   a patience
   b bitterness
   c cynicism
   d hatred

527. **Job and Zophar differed principally on whether**
              [Job 11:1, 6, 13–20; 12; 13:3, 13, 17–25]
   a God was fully aware of what He was doing to Job,
      and why
   b Job had brought this trouble on himself by his own
      wickedness

    c   Bildad was a less wicked man than Job

    d   Zophar had a more objective view of his own nature
          than Job had of his

528. **Said Job, "Wherefore do I take my flesh in my teeth,
and put my life in mine**   [Job 13:14]
    a   mouth?"
    b   cheek?"
    c   hand?"
    d   belly?"

529. **For man, lamented Job, there is less hope than for a**
                           [Job 14:7, 10–11, 18–19]
    a   tree
    b   mountain
    c   lake
    d   river

530. **Job's answer to Eliphaz's discourse does not include the
passage**   [Job 16, 17]
    a   "miserable comforters are ye all"
    b   "my breath is corrupt, my days are extinct"
    c   "He hath made me also a byword of the people"
    d   "I desire to reason with God"

531. **After Job's answer to Eliphaz, Bildad**   [Job 18:1, 5–21]
    a   showed Job some sympathy
    b   argued with his theology
    c   depicted vividly the fate of the wicked
    d   urged prayer to uncover the cause of Job's misfortune

532. **"I am escaped with the skin of my teeth," said**
                             [Job 19:1, 20]
    a   Bildad
    b   Eliphaz
    c   Job
    d   Zophar

533. **Zophar's second discourse paints the doom of the**
                             [Job 20]
    a   triumphant wicked
    b   desolate poor
    c   masochistic complainers
    d   manic adulterers

534. **"Mark me, and be astonished, and lay your hand upon
your mouth," said**   [Job 21:1, 5]
    a   Bildad
    b   Eliphaz
    c   Job
    d   Zophar

535. **Job's second reply to Zophar is concerned with the**
                            [Job 21:1, 7–33]
    a   prosperity and well-being of the wicked
    b   crushing burdens of the poor

c bodily ailments of the aged
d sexual distractions of the young

536. **The third discourse of Eliphaz**   [Job 22:1, 5–11]
a urges Job to be of good cheer
b accuses Job of infinite iniquities
c assures Job of his sympathy
d reveals how appalled he is

537. **Job then complains that**   [Job 23:1, 3–9]
a he cannot get in touch with God
b God does not listen
c God refutes all his arguments
d God punishes him for daring to present his case

538. **Bildad's third discourse differs from his first two in emphasizing the**   [Job 25:1, 4–6; see Job 8, 18]
a unrighteousness of all men rather than of Job
b iniquities peculiar to Job rather than to mankind
c hopelessness, rather than the injustice, of Job's position
d inappropriateness, rather than the ineffectiveness, of Job's complaints

539. **Wisdom, Job realized, is**   [Job 28:28]
a sympathy for the poor
b distrust of the rich
c fear of the Lord
d horror of Satan

540. **Job was deeply concerned over the loss of respect**
          [Job 29:1, 7–25; 30:1–15]
a of God for him
b of his fellow men for him
c by him, of his fellow men
d of Bildad for Eliphaz

541. **Elihu also was angry at Eliphaz, Bildad, and Zophar because they had**   [Job 32:1–3]
a ignored him, yet spoke to each other
b found no answer, yet condemned Job
c talked interminably, yet repeated themselves
d disagreed, yet misunderstood

542. **Elihu had hesitated to speak because he was** [Job 32:4–6]
a of a different tribe from Job
b not well trained in doctrine
c younger than Job's three friends
d burdened with a speech impediment

543. **Elihu was angry with Job because Job**
          [Job 33:8–12; 34:37; 32:1–2]
a justified himself
b bore himself too meekly

    c   argued with his friends
    d   cursed his fate

544.   **The notion that a person has a right to be better off if he has not sinned seemed to Elihu to be**   [Job 35:1–16]
    a   eminently justified
    b   acceptable
    c   questionable
    d   presumptuous

545.   **Elihu declared that if those who are afflicted listen to God's instructions to return from iniquity and serve Him, they**   [Job 36:1, 8–11]
    a   will nevertheless remain afflicted
    b   may nevertheless remain afflicted
    c   may spend their days in prosperity and their years in pleasures
    d   shall spend their days in prosperity and their years in pleasures

546.   **"Canst thou bind the sweet influences of Pleiades, or loose the bands of Orion?" asked**   [Job 38:1, 31]
    a   the Lord of Job
    b   Job of Elihu
    c   Elihu of Bildad
    d   Job of the Lord

547.   **Job, after the long discourse by the Lord,**
                                        [Job 40:3–5]
    a   upbraided Him for harshness
    b   complained that He was unjust
    c   acknowledged point by point the justice of His remarks
    d   said he would hold his tongue

548.   **Job's reaction to God's discourse was one of**
                                        [Job 42:1–6]
    a   utter terror
    b   stiff-necked pride
    c   repentance and self-abhorrence
    d   stupor

549.   **As to Eliphaz, Bildad, and Zophar, the Lord expressed Himself as**   [Job 42:7–9]
    a   displeased
    b   pleased
    c   indifferent
    d   puzzled

550.   **In conclusion, the Lord gave Job twice as much as he had before, in**   [Job 42:10, 12; 1:3]
    a   animals
    b   servants
    c   sons and daughters
    d   friends

551. **Jemima was**   [Job 42:13–15]
      a Job's new wife
      b Job's daughter
      c Kezia's daughter
      d Job's sister

Psalms

552. **The first Psalm**   [Psalms 1]
      a warns the kings of the earth
      b expresses trust in the Lord's protection
      c contrasts the futures of the righteous and the un-
         godly
      d exhorts against sin

553. **David, who was rebuked by the Lord for shedding so
      much blood (see No. 457), sings in the fifth Psalm that the
      Lord**   [Psalms 5:6]
      a encourages battle against worshipers of Baal
      b- abhors the bloody and deceitful man
      c smites those who invade His temple
      d pities the ignorant and overzealous

554. **In the sixth Psalm, David begs the Lord to save his life
      because he**   [Psalms 6:5]
      a fears the darkness hereafter
      b can then slay more of the wicked
      c can complete the building of the temple
      d cannot thank the Lord when he is dead

555. **David, in the eighth Psalm, praises the Lord for having
      made man**   [Psalms 8:5]
      a equal to the angels
      b a little lower than the angels
      c considerably lower than the angels
      d far lower than the angels

556. **"The wicked walk on every side," says the twelfth Psalm,
      when**   [Psalms 12:8]
      a "in arrogance the wicked pursue the poor"
      b "their throat is an open sepulchre"
      c "they have all gone astray"
      d "the vilest men are exalted"

557. **"Keep me as the apple of the eye," that is,**
                                                   [Psalms 17:8–9]
      a proud in the priesthood

b   secure in the afterlife
c   safe from my enemies
d   righteous in justice

558. **In the eighteenth Psalm David gives thanks to the Lord for enabling him to**   [Psalms 18:3–6, 16–19, 37–48]
a   prevent domestic discord
b   advance learning and the arts
c   reduce the inequality of incomes
d   rout his enemies

559. **"He teacheth my hands to war," so that "by mine arms," there is broken "a bow of**   [Psalms 18:34]
a   oak"
b   copper"
c   iron"
d   steel"

560. **That which "is as a bridegroom coming out of his chamber, and rejoiceth as a strong man to run a race" is the**   [Psalms 19:4–5]
a   mountain stream
b   thunderstorm
c   pine tree
d   sun

561. **The twenty-second Psalm opens with**   [Psalms 22:1–2]
a   a cry of anguish
b   a paean of praise
c   an appreciation of nature
d   a defiance of enemies

562. **In the twenty-third Psalm the analogy of the shepherd is carried through the**   [Psalms 23:1–6]
a   entire Psalm
b   first two-thirds
c   first third
d   first sentence only

563. **In the twenty-third Psalm David's enemies play a role that is**   [Psalms 23:1–6]
a   dominant
b   pervasive
c   muted
d   nil

564. **"The Lord is my light and my salvation" is in the**   [Psalms   :1]
a   26th Psalm
b   27th Psalm
c   28th Psalm
d   68th Psalm

565. **"The Lord is my strength and my shield" is in the**   [Psalms   :7]
a   26th Psalm

b   27th Psalm
c   28th Psalm
d   68th Psalm

566. **The thirty-first Psalm is an appeal for**   [Psalms 31:2–15]
a   rescue
b   forgiveness
c   bounty
d   credibility

567. **The thirty-second Psalm is an appeal for**
[Psalms 32:1, 3–5]
a   rescue
b   forgiveness
c   bounty
d   credibility

568. **In the thirty-fifth Psalm David asks that his enemies be**
[Psalms 35:4, 26]
a   forgiven
b   reformed
c   identified
d   put to shame

569. **The long thirty-seventh Psalm does not promise the right-eous, the perfect man, that he will**
[Psalms 37, especially 3, 9, 11, 19, 22, 28–29, 34]
a   inherit the earth
b   not have his posterity cut off
c   enjoy life after death
d   in days of famine be satisfied

570. **"For I am a stranger with thee, and a sojourner, as all my fathers were. O spare me, that I may recover strength, before I go hence,**   [Psalms 39:12–13]
a   for the life everlasting"
b   to descend to hell"
c   to join my forebears"
d   and be no more"

571. **"Deep calleth unto deep**   [Psalms 42:7]
a   through thy waves and billows"
b   within our souls"
c   at the noise of thy waterspouts"
d   in the rush of great waters"

572. **"Awake, why sleepest thou,**   [Psalms 44:23]
a   O Lord?"
b   O Israel?"
c   O David?"
d   O nations?"

573. **The fifty-first Psalm was composed by David**
[Psalms 51:Title]
a   when he feigned madness before Abimelech
b   when the Lord delivered him from the hand of Saul

c   when he sang to the Lord concerning Cush a Benjamite
d   after he had gone in to Bathsheba

574. **"The sacrifices of God are**   [Psalms 51:17]
a   a burnt offering"
b   truth in the inward being"
c   a broken spirit"
d   to teach transgressors thy ways"

575. **David sang, "Oh that I had wings like a dove!" that he
might**   [Psalms 55:6–8]
a   bring peace
b   be at rest
c   soar upward
d   make music

576. **"Deliver me from mine enemies, O my God," sang
David, when**   [Psalms 59:Title; 1]
a   the Philistines seized him in Gath
b   he fled from Saul, in the cave
c   Saul sent, and they watched the house to kill him
d   he strove with Aram-naharaim

577. **"Moab," said David, "is my**   [Psalms 60:8]
a   washpot"
b   helmet"
c   citadel"
d   courier"

578. **The phrase, "we went through fire and through water"
is found in Psalms**   [Psalms   :12]
a   65
b   66
c   67
d   68

579. **The phrase, "cause his face to shine upon us" is found in
Psalms**   [Psalms   :1]
a   65
b   66
c   67
d   68

580. **The phrase "his enemies shall lick the dust" is found in
a Psalm for**   [Psalms 72:Title; 9]
a   Asaph
b   David
c   Solomon
d   sons of Korah

581. **"Their eyes stand out with fatness," refers to**
[Psalms 73:3–12]
a   warriors
b   priests

  c old men
  d the wicked rich

582. **The seventy-eighth Psalm is a**   [Psalms 78]
  a lamentation
  b prophecy
  c recapitulation
  d denial

583. **Those who "go from strength to strength" are those who**
                                                  [Psalms 84:5–7]
  a have strength that is in God
  b have helped the children of Lot
  c sing aloud to God
  d alternate steadfast love and faithfulness

584. **David's prayer in the eighty-sixth Psalm is to be saved from**   [Psalms 86:14]
  a assemblies of violent men
  b eternal damnation
  c his own selfishness
  d ostracism .

585. **The eighty-eighth Psalm is one of the most**
                                                  [Psalms 88]
  a joyful
  b despairing
  c contentious
  d adoring

586. **The eighty-ninth Psalm charges the Lord with**
                                                  [Psalms 89:39]
  a neglecting His faithful
  b scattering His favors
  c making void the covenant
  d encouraging the wicked

587. **"For a thousand years . . . are but as yesterday" in the sight of**   [Psalms 90:1, 4]
  a Satan
  b the Lord
  c the faithful
  d the sinner in hell

588. **The ninetieth Psalm sets man's normal life span at**
                                                  [Psalms 90:10]
  a threescore and ten
  b fourscore
  c fourscore and ten
  d one hundred and twenty

589. **"Let the floods**   [Psalms 98:8]
  a sing for joy"
  b clap their hands"
  c rejoice"
  d be glad"

590. **The one hundred and first Psalm does not inveigh against the man who** [Psalms 101, especially 5, 7]
    a privily slandereth his neighbor
    b hath an high look and a proud heart
    c worketh deceit
    d seteth his mouth against the heavens

591. **"My bones," says one afflicted,** [Psalms 102:3]
    a "rattle like a gourd"
    b "crack like dried clay"
    c "are burned as an hearth"
    d "melt like wax"

592. **That the Lord deals with us according to our sins and rewards us according to our iniquities is, says the one hundred and third Psalm,** [Psalms 103:10]
    a true
    b not true
    c uncertain
    d unanswerable

593. **The one hundred and fourth Psalm is a paean to the Lord's** [Psalms 104:2–30]
    a propensity to forgive
    b creative power
    c love
    d patience

594. **The stork, says the one hundred and fourth Psalm, has her house in the** [Psalms 104:17]
    a cedars
    b cypresses
    c fir trees
    d palm trees

595. **"The young lions roar after their prey, and seek their meat from** [Psalms 104:21]
    a man"
    b their kind"
    c the sea"
    d God"

596. **"The beginning of wisdom" is** [Psalms 111:2, 5, 7, 10]
    a "the works of the Lord"
    b "His covenant"
    c "verity and judgment"
    d "the fear of the Lord"

597. **In the one hundred and twelfth Psalm, the rewards to the man "that feareth the Lord, that delighteth greatly in his commandments" do not include the following:** [Psalms 112, especially 2, 3]
    a his seed shall be mighty upon earth
    b wealth and riches shall be in his house
    c he shall have a life after death
    d his righteousness shall endure forever

598. **The other nations' idols are not the true God, says the one hundred and fifteenth Psalm, for**   [Psalms 115:2–8]
    a they foster cruelty
    b their bodily organs are nonfunctional
    c they err constantly in their prophesying
    d they differ, nation to nation

599. **"The stone which the builders refused is become the**
                                                        [Psalms 118:22]
    a scorn of mankind"
    b stone of the roadway"
    c instrument of disaster"
    d head stone of the corner"

600. **By far the most lengthy of all the Psalms, the hundred and nineteenth,**   [Psalms 119]
    a recounts the history of Israel from Joseph to David
    b lists the punishments that await the wicked
    c describes the sanctuary
    d praises the Lord's laws and commandments

601. **"Sharp arrows of the mighty, with coals of juniper" shall be the penalty for**   [Psalms 120:2–4]
    a lustful eyes
    b a grasping hand
    c a deceitful tongue
    d arrogant elbows

602. **"As arrows are in the hand of a mighty man; so are**
                                                        [Psalms 127:4]
    a water-courses of the Negeb"
    b mountains about Jerusalem"
    c enemies at the gate"
    d children of the youth"

603. **"It is like the precious ointment upon the head, that ran down upon the beard," when**   [Psalms 133:1–2]
    a brethren dwell in unity
    b tribes dwell in unity
    c nations dwell in unity
    d the insolent are laid low

604. **The King of Bashan was**   [Psalms 135:11]
    a Ag
    b Eg
    c Ig
    d Og

605. **"By the rivers of Babylon, there we sat down, yea, we**
                                                        [Psalms 137:1]
    a wept"
    b cried"
    c lamented"
    d grieved"

606. **The Psalmist is bitter, in the one hundred and thirty-
seventh Psalm, because the captors of the Israelites**
[Psalms 137:3]
  a   refused to let them sing the songs of Zion
  b   themselves sang the songs of Zion
  c   compelled them to sing a song of Zion
  d   were not aware of the songs of Zion

607. **"Happy shall he be," says the Psalmist, who takes your
little ones and**   [Psalms 137:9]
  a   dashes them against the stones
  b   raises them in the faith of Israel
  c   sends them into exile
  d   sells them as slaves

608. **The one hundred and thirty-ninth Psalm is in praise of
God's**   [Psalms 139]
  a   omnipotence
  b   omniscience
  c   omnipresence
  d   omnifariousness

609. **"Let the righteous smite me; it shall be**   [Psalms 141:5]
  a   a kindness" ,
  b   an outrage"
  c   a reproach"
  d   a sorrow"

610. **In the one hundred and forty-fourth Psalm, David re-
quests that there may be as "corner stones, polished
after the similitude of a palace," our**   [Psalms 144:12]
  a   sons
  b   daughters
  c   brothers
  d   parents

611. **In describing God's control of the weather, the Psalmist
does not refer to**   [Psalms 147:8–18, especially 8, 16, 18]
  a   winds
  b   clouds
  c   snow
  d   thunder

612. **In commanding the elements to praise the Lord, the
Psalmist does not refer to**   [Psalms 148:8]
  a   winds
  b   clouds
  c   snow
  d   hail

The Proverbs

613. **The Proverbs are entitled, in 1:1, the proverbs of**
[Proverbs 1:1]
   a David
   b Ethan
   c Isaiah
   d Solomon

614. **"The beginning of knowledge" is** [Proverbs 1:3, 6–8]
   a "the words of the wise"
   b "justice, and judgment, and equity"
   c "the fear of the Lord"
   d "the instruction of thy father"

615. **"Wisdom is the principal thing; therefore**
[Proverbs 4:7, 11; 3:13, 21]
   a get wisdom: and with all thy getting get understanding"
   b I have taught thee in the way of wisdom"
   c keep sound wisdom and discretion"
   d happy is the man that findeth wisdom"

616. **"The lips of a strange woman [loose woman] drop as**
[Proverbs 5:3]
   a oil"
   b bitterness"
   c an honeycomb"
   d slander"

617. **"As the loving hind and pleasant roe," let be the**
[Proverbs 5:18–19]
   a "spirit of wisdom"
   b "wife of thy youth"
   c "sister thou hast"
   d "spirit of insight"

618. **"Go to the ant, thou sluggard;" because she**
[Proverbs 6:6–8]
   a epitomizes cooperative labor
   b spends all her waking hours in work
   c drags objects many times her weight
   d anticipates her needs

619. **"Yet a little sleep, a little slumber, a little folding of the hands to sleep," and there follows** [Proverbs 6:10–11]
   a bodily decay
   b poverty and want
   c illicit thoughts
   d contentment

620. **"As an ox goeth to the slaughter," so goes the**
[Proverbs 7:7–22]

    a   arrogant to the court of justice
    b   spendthrift to the moneylender
    c   young man to the harlot
    d   desperate to the diamond mines

621. **The eighth chapter is a paean to**   [Proverbs 8]
    a   courage
    b   wisdom
    c   love
    d   resignation

622. **Wisdom, says the ninth chapter, hath**   [Proverbs 9:1]
    a   four pillars
    b   seven pillars
    c   thirteen pillars
    d   forty pillars

623. **Do not, says the ninth chapter, reprove the**
[Proverbs 9:8–9]

    a   wise
    b   righteous
    c   scornful
    d   ignorant

624. **The tenth chapter declares that**
[Proverbs 10:1, 2, 4, 12]
    a   a wise son maketh a glad mother
    b   a slack hand causeth bodily harm
    c   treasures of wickedness bringeth trouble
    d   love covereth all sins

625. **"The destruction of the poor" is their**   [Proverbs 10:15]
    a   slothfulness
    b   ignorance
    c   rudeness
    d   poverty

626. **"He that hateth suretiship is**   [Proverbs 11:15]
    a   selfish"
    b   simple"
    c   sure"
    d   savage"

627. **"As a jewel of gold in a swine's snout" is a**
[Proverbs 11:22]

    a   diligent woman without sense
    b   fair woman without discretion
    c   single woman without envy
    d   intelligent woman without beauty

628. **"The ransom of a man's life are his**   [Proverbs 13:8]
    a   children"
    b   hopes"

    c forebears"
    d riches"

629. **"Wealth gotten by vanity**   [Proverbs 13:11]
    a earns interest"
    b destroys health"
    c shall be diminished"
    d implies knavery"

630. **"Hope deferred maketh the**   [Proverbs 13:12]
    a mind boggle"
    b heart sick"
    c soul patient"
    d spirit tough"

631. **"He that spareth his rod**   [Proverbs 13:24]
    a spoileth the child"
    b loveth his son"
    c hateth his son"
    d feareth his child"

632. **"The end of that mirth is**   [Proverbs 14:13]
    a contentment"
    b wisdom"
    c apathy"
    d heaviness"

633. **He who is "hated even of his own neighbour" and he who "hath many friends" are, respectively, the**
                       [Proverbs 14:20]
    a poor and the rich
    b rich and the poor
    c simple and the wise
    d wise and the simple

634. **"A soft answer turneth away**   [Proverbs 15:1]
    a envy"
    b wrath"
    c importunity"
    d hate"

635. **The Lord hath made the wicked for**   [Proverbs 16:4]
    a an example to the wise
    b salvation by repentance
    c the day of evil
    d no apparent purpose

636. **"Pride goeth before**   [Proverbs 16:18]
    a humiliation"
    b a fall"
    c destruction"
    d poverty"

637. **The sixteenth chapter declares that**   [Proverbs 16:24]
    a honey catches more flies than vinegar
    b bees have more friends than ants

    c   pleasant words are like a honeycomb
    d   persuasive speech drips like honey

638. **"He that is slow to anger is**   [Proverbs 16:32]
    a   asking for trouble"
    b   loved by all"
    c   better than the mighty"
    d   torpid in spirit"

639. **"The words of a talebearer are as**   [Proverbs 18:8]
    a   poisonous juices"
    b   bitter herbs"
    c   wounds"
    d   strong drink"

640. **"Whoso findeth a wife findeth**   [Proverbs 18:22]
    a   trouble"
    b   help"
    c   a good thing"
    d   himself"

641. **"The poor useth entreaties; but the rich answereth**
                          [Proverbs 18:23]
    a   generously"
    b   carefully"
    c   ambiguously"
    d   roughly"

642. **"Chasten thy son while there is hope, and let not thy soul spare for his**   [Proverbs 19:18]
    a   love"
    b   advancement"
    c   companionship"
    d   crying"

643. **"Divers weights, and divers measures"** [Proverbs 20:10]
    a   "afford the seller many pleasures"
    b   "are alike abomination to the Lord"
    c   "reflect variety in human experience"
    d   "will never bring the merchant treasures"

644. **"Labour not to be**   [Proverbs 23:4]
    a   respected"
    b   powerful"
    c   inconspicuous"
    d   rich"

645. **"Eat thou not the bread of him that hath**
                          [Proverbs 23:6]
    a   an evil eye"
    b   a loose tongue"
    c   a rapacious spirit"
    d   a poor cook"

646. **"Buy the truth, and**   [Proverbs 23:23]
    a   steal it not"

    b beg it not"
    c scorn it not"
    d sell it not"

647. **"If thou forbear to deliver them that are drawn unto death, and those that are ready to be slain," do not seek to excuse yourself by saying that you**
[Proverbs 24:11–12]
    a thought they were evildoers
    b were too weak
    c did not know of it
    d expected the same fate

648. **"Rejoice not when thine enemy falleth," lest**
[Proverbs 24:17–18]
    a the Lord turn away His wrath from him
    b your spirit become corrupt
    c you be premature in your joy
    d he recover and seek revenge

649. **The principle of "I will do so to him as he hath done to me" is, in chapter 24,**   [Proverbs 24:29]
    a approved
    b suggested
    c dismissed
    d condemned

650. **"Whoso boasteth himself of a false gift is like**
[Proverbs 25:14]
    a the cold of snow"
    b a sharp arrow"
    c a bad tooth"
    d clouds and wind without rain"

651. **"Withdraw thy foot from thy neighbour's house; lest he**
[Proverbs 25:17]
    a ask thee for money"
    b be weary of thee"
    c plan for a dowry"
    d set foot in thine"

652. **"He that singeth songs to an heavy heart" is as**
[Proverbs 25:20]
    a "honey upon bread"
    b "salve upon a wound"
    c "vinegar upon nitre"
    d "gold upon lead"

653. **"For thou shalt heap coals of fire upon his head" by giving a thirsty enemy**   [Proverbs 25:21–22]
    a water to drink
    b nothing to drink
    c just a little to drink
    d salt

654. **"It is better to dwell in the corner of the housetop than
     with a**   [Proverbs 25:24]
     a   sluggard wife"
     b   wicked brother"
     c   brawling woman"
     d   poor man"

655. **"As a dog returneth to his vomit, so**   [Proverbs 26:11]
     a   a sluggard returneth to his couch"
     b   an unbeliever returneth to his idols"
     c   a fool returneth to his folly"
     d   a talebearer returneth to his gossip"

656. **"Who is able to stand before**   [Proverbs 27:4]
     a   anger?"
     b   hatred?"
     c   envy?"
     d   wrath?"

657. **Better is**   [Proverbs 27:5]
     a   open rebuke than secret love
     b   secret love than open rebuke
     c   open love than secret rebuke
     d   secret rebuke than open love

658. **"He that blesseth his friend with a loud voice, rising
     early in the morning, it shall be counted a**
                                       [Proverbs 27:14]
     a   joy to him"
     b   courtesy to him"
     c   bother to him"
     d   curse to him"

659. **A contentious woman is like a continual**
                                       [Proverbs 27:15-16]
     a   breaking of the surf upon the shore
     b   itching on a warm and humid day
     c   biting from a cloud of tiny flies
     d   dropping in a very rainy day

660. **"The wicked flee when**   [Proverbs 28:1]
     a   the righteous pursueth"
     b   the wicked pursueth"
     c   the Lord pursueth"
     d   no man pursueth"

661. **Like "a sweeping rain, which leaveth no food" is a**
                                       [Proverbs 28:3]
     a   poor man that oppresseth the poor
     b   rich man that oppresseth the poor
     c   poor man that oppresseth the rich
     d   rich man that oppresseth the rich

662. **"The rod and reproof give**   [Proverbs 29:15]
     a   sorrow"
     b   trauma"

    c wisdom"
    d caution"

663. **"He that delicately bringeth up his servant from a child shall have him become his**   [Proverbs 29:21]
    a bodyguard"
    b ruler"
    c friend"
    d son"

664. **The four things that Agur son of Jakeh found too wonderful for him did not include the way of**
[Proverbs 30:18–19]
    a an eagle in the air
    b a serpent in the pool
    c a ship in the midst of the sea
    d a man with a maid

665. **"There be four things which are little upon the earth, but they are exceeding wise:"**   [Proverbs 30:24–28]
    a ants, conies, locusts, spiders
    b ants, gnats, lizards, locusts
    c conies, gnats, locusts, spiders
    d ants, conies, lizards, spiders

666. **Chapter 31 is devoted chiefly to the**
[Proverbs 31:10–31]
    a obedient child
    b industrious husband
    c good wife
    d loving mother

Ecclesiastes

667. **"All is vanity," says the Preacher; that is, no one**
[Ecclesiastes 1:2–4]
    a is modest
    b obtains what he aims at
    c profits by labor
    d takes pleasure in serious matters

668. **"There is no new thing under the sun," says the Preacher, because all things**   [Ecclesiastes 1:9–10]
    a are of equal worth
    b that have been, will be
    c have been used by others
    d in the sun's glare appear alike

669. **"He that increaseth knowledge increaseth**
[Ecclesiastes 1:18]
   a   power"
   b   sorrow"
   c   arrogance"
   d   confusion"

670. **Chapter 2 suggests that all in all the best is**
[Ecclesiastes 2:24–26]
   a   consumption
   b   saving
   c   idleness
   d   labour

671. **In chapter 3 the Preacher did not say that there is a time**   [Ecclesiastes 3:2–9, especially 2, 5, 6]
   a   to be born and a time to die
   b   to get and a time to lose
   c   to lie and a time to speak the truth
   d   to embrace and a time to refrain from embracing

672. **Two are**   [Ecclesiastes 4:9–12]
   a   equal to one
   b   better than one
   c   worse than one
   d   just twice one

673. **"God is in heaven, and thou upon earth: therefore let thy words be**   [Ecclesiastes 5:2]
   a   few"
   b   many"
   c   well chosen"
   d   spoken clearly"

674. **"He that loveth silver shall not be satisfied with**
[Ecclesiastes 5:10]
   a   silver"
   b   love"
   c   power"
   d   knowledge"

675. **"Surely oppression maketh a wise man**
[Ecclesiastes 7:7]
   a   wiser"
   b   strong"
   c   mad"
   d   reckless"

676. **The Preacher, in chapter 7, seems on the whole to regard women with**   [Ecclesiastes 7:26–28]
   a   affection
   b   admiration
   c   apprehension
   d   ambiguity

677. **"A living dog is better than**   [Ecclesiastes 9:4]
    a   a dead lion"
    b   a dead dog"
    c   a living lion"
    d   an unborn dog"

678. **"Under the sun," says the Preacher, "the race is**
                                     [Ecclesiastes 9:11]
    a   to the swift"
    b   not to the swift"
    c   alternately yes and no to the swift"
    d   to the slow"

679. **"The poor man's wisdom is**   [Ecclesiastes 9:16]
    a   rare"
    b   homely"
    c   despised"
    d   prized"

680. **The Preacher implies that a little folly stinks more if it comes from a**   [Ecclesiastes 10:1]
    a   fool
    b   madman
    c   wise man
    d   stranger

681. **"Money answereth**   [Ecclesiastes 10:19]
    a   nothing"
    b   all things"
    c   sin"
    d   money"

682. **"Curse not the king, no not in thy thought; and curse not the rich in thy bedchamber," because it**
                                    [Ecclesiastes 10:20]
    a   is unseemly
    b   is uncharitable
    c   will become known
    d   can be corroding

683. **"Cast thy bread upon the waters," because you**
                                    [Ecclesiastes 11:1]
    a   will enjoy being generous
    b   cannot live by bread alone
    c   can thus tame the waters
    d   will find it after many days

684. **"Of making many books there is**   [Ecclesiastes 12:12]
    a   little profit"
    b   no end"
    c   great folly"
    d   great glory"

Song of Solomon

685. **"I am the rose of Sharon, and the lily of the valleys."**
And "my love among the daughters" is as a lily among
[Song of Solomon 2:1–2]

    a   lilies
    b   crocuses
    c   thorns
    d   spikenard

686. **"Stay me with flagons, comfort me with apples: for**
[Song of Solomon 2:5; 5:1; 7:7, 13]

    a   I am come into my garden, my sister, my spouse"
    b   thy stature is like to a palm tree, and thy breasts
        to clusters of grapes"
    c   at our gates are all manner of pleasant fruits, new and
        old"
    d   I am sick of love"

687. **"The voice of the turtle is heard in our land," for it is**
[Song of Solomon 2:11–12]

    a   spring
    b   summer
    c   autumn
    d   winter

688. **"Take us the foxes, the little foxes, that**
[Song of Solomon 2:15, 8–9; 1:8]

    a   skip upon the hills"
    b   looketh forth at the windows"
    c   spoil the vines: for our vines have tender grapes"
    d   go forth thy way by the footsteps of the flock"

689. **Sings the man to his beloved, "thy**
[Song of Solomon 4:1; 5:13, 15]

    a   cheeks are as a bed of spices"
    b   lips like lilies"
    c   legs are as pillars of marble"
    d   hair is as a flock of goats"

690. **Sings the woman to her beloved, thy**
[Song of Solomon 5:14; 4:4, 12]

    a   "teeth are like a flock of sheep that are even shorn"
    b   "neck is like the tower of David"
    c   "hair is as a flock of goats"
    d   "hands are as gold rings set with the beryl"

691. **The man to his beloved: "Thy belly is like**
[Song of Solomon 7:1–2, 4; 5:14]

    a   a rounded goblet"

    b   an heap of wheat set about with lilies"
    c   the tower of Lebanon"
    d   bright ivory"

692. **In the last chapter of the Song of Solomon the daughters of Jerusalem are once more adjured, "stir not up, nor awake my love, until**
                        [Song of Solomon 8:4; 2:17; 6:2; 7:13]
    a   he has gone down into his garden"
    b   the day break and the shadows flee away"
    c   he please"
    d   the mandrakes give a smell"

693. **In the Song of Solomon we hear**   [Song of Solomon]
    a   only a man
    b   only a woman
    c   a man and a woman
    d   more than one man and one woman

Isaiah

694. **In the vision that Isaiah had of Judah and Jerusalem, the Lord said that of burnt offerings of rams and the fat of fed beasts He desired**   [Isaiah 1:1, 11]
    a   more
    b   no more
    c   the same
    d   any given amount

695. **The nations "shall beat their swords into plowshares, and their spears into**   [Isaiah 2:4]
    a   fenceposts"
    b   spades"
    c   garden hoes"
    d   pruninghooks"

696. **"What mean ye that ye . . . grind the faces of the poor?" said**   [Isaiah 3:15]
    a   Isaiah
    b   Uzziah
    c   the Lord God of hosts
    d   Amoz

697. **The Lord inveighed against the daughters of Zion who walked with necks**   [Isaiah 3:16]
    a   laid bare
    b   gold hooped

    c   perfumed
    d   stretched forth

698. **As to such daughters of Zion, the Lord declared He would discover their** [Isaiah 3:17]
    a   heads
    b   eyes
    c   minds
    d   secret parts

699. **Isaiah's prophecy was of the destruction of Judah by** [Isaiah 7:17–20; 8:4, 7–8]
    a   Babylon
    b   Assyria
    c   Persia
    d   Ethiopia

700. **"Shall the axe boast itself against him that heweth therewith?" said the Lord, referring to** [Isaiah 10:12–13, 15]
    a   Judah
    b   David
    c   Carchemish
    d   King of Assyria

701. **The prophet Isaiah foresaw for Israel** [Isaiah 10:20–22]
    a   permanent destruction
    b   near destruction, then return of a remnant
    c   near destruction, then complete recoupment
    d   partial destruction, then complete recoupment

702. **"And a little child shall lead them," said Isaiah, referring to** [Isaiah 11:6]
    a   Assyrians
    b   exiles
    c   prophets
    d   animals

703. **"The wolf," said Isaiah, "shall** [Isaiah 11:6]
    a   dwell with the lamb"
    b   lie down with the kid"
    c   eat with the fatling"
    d   hunt with the leopard"

704. **"Wild beasts of the islands shall cry in their desolate houses, and dragons in their pleasant palaces," said Isaiah of** [Isaiah 13:1, 22]
    a   Jerusalem
    b   Cairo
    c   Babylon
    d   Nineveh

705. **Isaiah predicted that Damascus would become** [Isaiah 17:1]
    a   the salvation of the Israelites

    b   a ruinous heap
    c   the conqueror of Judah
    d   a many-storied splendor

706. **The Lord "rideth upon a swift cloud, and shall come into Egypt," and the river shall** [Isaiah 19:1, 5]
    a   flood the land
    b   run uphill
    c   be wasted and dried up
    d   turn to blood

707. **"In that day shall there be a highway out of** [Isaiah 19:23]
    a   Egypt to Assyria"
    b   Egypt to Israel"
    c   Israel to Assyria"
    d   Babylon to Egypt"

708. **Sargon was** [Isaiah 20:1]
    a   King of Egypt
    b   King of Assyria
    c   commander-in-chief of Assyria
    d   a rare gas

709. **Isaiah's walking naked and barefoot for three years was a portent that** [Isaiah 20:2–4]
    a   Assyria would lead away Egyptians and Ethiopians
    b   Egypt would lead away Assyrians and Ethiopians
    c   Ethiopia would lead away Assyrians and Egyptians
    d   all three would lead away Israel

710. **"Arise, ye princes, and anoint the** [Isaiah 21:5]
    a   chariot"
    b   spear"
    c   bow"
    d   shield"

711. **"Fallen, is fallen," is** [Isaiah 21:6–9]
    a   Jerusalem
    b   Babylon
    c   Nineveh
    d   Tyre

712. **"Watchman, what of the night?" and the watchman replies,** [Isaiah 21:11–12]
    a   "Make your shade like the night at the height of the noon"
    b   "The night hath dispersed like the Hivites in battle"
    c   "The Assyrians came down like a night on the fold"
    d   "The morning cometh, and also the night"

713. **"Let us eat and drink, for to morrow we shall die," said those whom the Lord had** [Isaiah 22:12–13]
    a   threatened with destruction
    b   called to weeping and to mourning

    c   sent against Assyria
    d   ordered to fast

714. **In "Howl, ye ships of Tarshish; for it is laid waste," the "it" is**   [Isaiah 23:1]
    a   Jerusalem
    b   Babylon
    c   Nineveh
    d   Tyre

715. **Isaiah 24 is a prophecy of**   [Isaiah 24]
    a   elevation
    b   excitation
    c   oscillation
    d   desolation

716. **"Woe unto me!" says the prophet, for here the**
                                              [Isaiah 24:16]
    a   "evil dealers have dealt evilly"
    b   "vicious dealers have dealt viciously"
    c   "treacherous dealers have dealt treacherously"
    d   "unrighteous dealers have dealt unrighteously"

717. **"For precept must be upon precept, precept upon precept; line upon line, line upon line;**   [Isaiah 28:10, 13]
    a   sentence upon sentence"
    b   word upon word"
    c   here a little, and there a little"
    d   morning and noon, noon and night"

718. **"And thy speech shall whisper out of the dust," says Isaiah to Ariel (Jerusalem), before you are**
                                            [Isaiah 29:4–7]
    a   annihilated
    b   abandoned
    c   exiled
    d   rescued

719. **"In the day of the great slaughter, when the towers fall," there "shall be upon every high mountain, and upon every high hill, rivers and streams of**   [Isaiah 30:25]
    a   waters"
    b   blood"
    c   detritus"
    d   salt"

720. **In Isaiah 31 the Lord is likened to**   [Isaiah 31:4]
    a   a band of shepherds against a lion
    b   a lion against a band of shepherds
    c   a lion consorting with a band of shepherds
    d   a band of shepherds leading a lion

721. **In Isaiah 34, "the mountains shall be melted with their**
                                            [Isaiah 34:3]
    a   water"
    b   blood"

    c   pitch"
    d   salt"

722. **In Isaiah 34, "the streams thereof shall be turned into** [Isaiah 34:9]

    a   washes"
    b   blood"
    c   pitch"
    d   salt"

723. **"All flesh is** [Isaiah 40:6]

    a   dust"
    b   flower"
    c   grass"
    d   glass"

724. **The Lord, implies Isaiah, has** [Isaiah 40:12]

    a   marked off the waters with a span
    b   weighed the heavens in scales
    c   measured the mountains in the hollow of His hand
    d   comprehended the dust of the earth in a measure

725. **"Behold," says Isaiah, "as a drop of a bucket" are the** [Isaiah 40:15]

    a   nations
    b   rulers
    c   isles
    d   man

726. **"He feedeth on ashes" refers to the one who** [Isaiah 44:15–20]

    a   fasts in the worship of an idol
    b   does penance to the Lord
    c   roasts meat with the same wood that he worships
    d   approaches death

727. **The one who the Lord says is His anointed, "whose right hand I have holden, to subdue nations before him," is** [Isaiah 45:1]

    a   Jacob
    b   Cyrus
    c   Jeshurun
    d   Egypt

728. **"O virgin daughter of Babylon . . . these two things shall come to thee in a moment in one day":** [Isaiah 47:1, 9]

    a   disease and death
    b   rape and pregnancy
    c   loss of sight and failure of speech
    d   loss of children and widowhood

729. **"Thou art obstinate, and thy neck is an iron sinew, and thy brow brass," said the Lord, of** [Isaiah 48:1, 4]

    a   the virgin of Babylon
    b   the Israelites

    c   the Chaldeans
    d   Nebo

730. **The Lord deferred His anger against His erring people,**
                                     [Isaiah 48:9–11]
    a   out of sympathy for them
    b   for His name's sake
    c   to make His rule attractive
    d   to punish all the more severely later

731. **"Behold, I have graven thee upon the palms of my
hands," said the Lord to the people of Zion, indicating
that He**   [Isaiah 49:14–16]
    a   had held them in His grip
    b   could read their fortune
    c   would never forget them
    d   had often clasped hands

732. **For the eunuchs that take hold of His covenant, the Lord
promises, in Isaiah 56,**   [Isaiah 56:4–5]
    a   political power
    b   an everlasting name
    c   virility
    d   escape from hell

733. **"There is no peace," says God, "to the**   [Isaiah 57:21]
    a   defenseless"
    b   righteous"
    c   self-appointed"
    d   wicked"

734. **The brilliant future of Zion painted in Isaiah 60 does not
promise great achievements in**
                [Isaiah 60:5–22, especially 5–9, 13, 18]
    a   commerce
    b   architecture and decoration
    c   peacemaking
    d   science and scholarship

735. **The Lord's apparel is red, because**   [Isaiah 63:1–6]
    a   red symbolizes redemption, from the sunrise
    b   He will trample the peoples in His fury
    c   it recalls the crossing of the Red Sea
    d   red symbolizes peace, from the sundown

736. **In Isaiah 63, Isaiah asks the Lord why He** [Isaiah 63:17]
    a   becomes Israel's enemy merely because they rebelled
    b   has so often alternated between favor and fright-
        fulness
    c   has made the Israelites do the things He then pun-
        ishes them for
    d   has chosen Zion for rebuilding rather than a more
        promising site

737. **"I create new heavens and a new earth," says the Lord,
in which**   [Isaiah 65:17, 20, 25]

  a   the wolf and the lamb shall not feed together
  b   the lion shall not eat straw like the bullock
  c   the child shall die an hundred years old
  d   dust shall not be the serpent's meat

738. **In Isaiah 66, Jerusalem is likened to a**   [Isaiah 66:10–13]
  a   mother
  b   sister
  c   daughter
  d   mistress

Jeremiah

739. **The Lord told Jeremiah that backsliding Israel had justified herself, compared with treacherous Judah,**
                                              [Jeremiah 3:11]

  a   more
  b   equally
  c   less
  d   not at all

740. **"They were as fed horses in the morning: every one neighed after his**   [Jeremiah 5:8]
  a   measure of barley"
  b   warrior rider"
  c   neighbour's wife"
  d   master's mare"

741. **"A wonderful and horrible thing is committed in the land; the prophets**   [Jeremiah 5:30–31]
  a   prophesy falsely"
  b   practice apostasy"
  c   promise outrageously"
  d   meet with indifference"

742. **"They have healed also the hurt of the daughter of my people slightly," said the Lord, "saying Peace, peace; when there is no peace," because there is instead**
                             [Jeremiah 6:14, 22–23; 8:11]

  a   internal dissention
  b   external aggression
  c   psychic disorientation
  d   too much talk

743. **Tophet, says the Lord, has been built as a place for**
                                              [Jeremiah 7:31]

  a   drunken orgies

    b   human sacrifice
    c   the tabernacle
    d   launching ships

744. **"Is there no balm in Gilead?" Jeremiah asks, because**
                                          [Jeremiah 8:22]
    a   Gilead was known for its production of balm
    b   no one was ever comfortable in Gilead
    c   David hid from Absalom in Gilead
    d   "balm" is a corruption of "palm"

745. **In Jeremiah 9, the Lord's chief complaint against His people is that they are**   [Jeremiah 9:2-6, 8]
    a   lazy
    b   idolatrous
    c   untruthful
    d   lascivious

746. **Idols are not to be feared, says the Lord, offering as evidence the fact that they cannot**   [Jeremiah 10:5]
    a   walk
    b   feel
    c   touch
    d   sleep

747. **One of the doleful promises that the Lord relayed through Jeremiah was that the inhabitants of Jerusalem would be dashed one against the other, to their destruction, through**   [Jeremiah 13:13-14]
    a   drug addiction
    b   drunkenness
    c   mental illness
    d   diseases of the central nervous system

748. **Can the leopard change his spots? asks the Lord rhetorically, and the implied answer is**   [Jeremiah 13:23]
    a   yes
    b   no
    c   maybe
    d   no one knows

749. **In Jeremiah 13, the Lord's most forceful complaint against His people is that they are**   [Jeremiah 13:27]
    a   lazy
    b   idolatrous
    c   untruthful
    d   lascivious

750. **In the time of drought, Jeremiah despairingly asks the Lord, "Hast thou utterly rejected Judah? hath thy soul loathed Zion?" and the Lord's answer at first seems to imply**   [Jeremiah 14:1-6, 19; 15:1-4]
    a   of course not
    b   not really
    c   not quite yet
    d   yes, indeed

751. **As to pardoning these people, says the Lord:**
                                                [Jeremiah 15:6]
    a   I never repent
    b   I repent periodically
    c   I dislike to repent
    d   I am weary with repenting

752. **Along with His promises of destruction and exile the Lord gave His people, with respect to aid from Him in the future,**   [Jeremiah 16:11–15]
    a   no assurance
    b   qualified assurance
    c   unqualified assurance
    d   ambiguous promises

753. **"The sin of Judah," says the Lord, "is written with a pen of**   [Jeremiah 17:1]
    a   fire"
    b   iron"
    c   sulphur"
    d   diamond"

754. **In Jeremiah 17 the Lord promises a bright future for Judah if the people**   [Jeremiah 17:19–27]
    a   destroy their idols
    b   forgo adultery
    c   keep the Sabbath
    d   tell the truth

755. **As one of the retributions on the people of Jerusalem for, *inter alia,* having given their sons as burnt offerings to Baal, the Lord declared He would make them eat the flesh of their**   [Jeremiah 19:4–5, 9]
    a   sons and their daughters
    b   horses and camels
    c   burnt offerings of oxen
    d   enemies

756. **Pashur the son of Immer the priest put Jeremiah the prophet in**   [Jeremiah 20:2]
    a   prison
    b   the stocks
    c   exile
    d   a well

757. **By the time Nebuchadrezzar became King of Babylon, Jeremiah had been dispensing his warnings to the people of Judah for**   [Jeremiah 25:1–3]
    a   three years
    b   seven years
    c   sixteen years
    d   twenty-three years

758. **The Lord declared that after He had laid waste the land of Judah and of the nations round about, He would do**

the same to the land of the Chaldeans after an interval of
[Jeremiah 25:9–12]

a   seven years
b   seventy years
c   one hundred and seventy years
d   three hundred years

759. Jeremiah's gloomy prophecies led him to be threatened
with death by Judah's   [Jeremiah 26:7–19]
a   priests and prophets
b   princes and people
c   elders
d   enemies

760. The Lord declared that He would punish "with the sword,
and with the famine, and with the pestilence" that nation
that   [Jeremiah 27:8]
a   put its neck under the yoke of the King of Babylon
b   did not put its neck under the yoke of the King of
Babylon
c   put any other nation's neck under the yoke of the
King of Babylon
d   put the King of Babylon's neck under its yoke

761. In taking the yoke from off the neck of Jeremiah, the
Prophet Hananiah acted   [Jeremiah 28:10–17]
a   graciously
b   rudely
c   awkwardly
d   injudiciously

762. Jeremiah sent word to the exiles from Jerusalem in
Babylon to do what they could to   [Jeremiah 29:1, 7]
a   increase Babylon's peace
b   diminish Babylon's peace
c   refrain from influencing Babylon's peace
d   increase the peace of Babylon's competitors

763. "Ask ye now, and see whether a man doth travail with
child?" asks the Lord, implying that the men of Israel and
Judah were   [Jeremiah 30:5–6]
a   arrogant
b   terror stricken
c   confused
d   weak

764. The days are coming, declared the Lord, in Jeremiah 31,
when any man's teeth shall be set on edge if sour grapes
are eaten by   [Jeremiah 31:27–30]
a   him
b   his children
c   his father
d   his neighbor

765. **And in those days, added the Lord, every man shall teach his neighbor and every man his brother (saying, "Know the Lord"),**   [Jeremiah 31:34]
    a   when requested
    b   no more
    c   repeatedly
    d   as before

766. **The Lord caused land to be bought and sold, with deeds sealed and witnessed, in this area soon to be desolated, because He**   [Jeremiah 32:16-44]
    a   this way punished the evil doers
    b   distracted the peoples of Israel and Judah from con-templating their unpromising future
    c   was determined to restore the lands to the peoples of Israel and Judah
    d   thus emphasized the vanity of life

767. **In the assurances for the future of Israel and Judah that the Lord gave to Jeremiah when he was shut up in the court of the prison, the Lord emphasized His covenant with**   [Jeremiah 33:1, 15-22]
    a   Abraham
    b   Jacob
    c   David
    d   Solomon

768. **"Thou shalt not die by the sword: But thou shalt die in peace," said the Lord to the sinful King Zedekiah of Judah (through Jeremiah), omitting to add that his Babylonian captors would**
                    [Jeremiah 34:2-5; 39:4-7; 2 Kings 25:7]
    a   starve him
    b   blind him
    c   deny him medical aid
    d   work him to death

769. **A six-year limit on the service of a Hebrew who had been sold to a fellow Hebrew had been, in the eyes of the Lord,**   [Jeremiah 34:8-15]
    a   too long
    b   acceptable
    c   too short
    d   wrong in principle

770. **The Rechabites' refusal to drink wine, build a house, sow seed or plant a vineyard was evidently, in the view of the Lord,**   [Jeremiah 35:5-19]
    a   commendable
    b   understandable
    c   untenable
    d   abominable

771. **Baruch's task was to**   [Jeremiah 36:4-8]
    a   assemble the princes

b   raise funds
c   write, and read aloud
d   conduct services

772. **The scroll on which Baruch, upon dictation by Jeremiah, at the Lord's command, wrote all the words He had spoken to him against Israel and Judah and the other nations, was read to King Jehoiakim of Judah, who, upon hearing a few pages of it,** [Jeremiah 36:1–4, 22–23]
a   ordered its contents translated into the vernacular
b   had it nailed to the otuside of his door
c   cut it with a penknife and cast it into the fire on the hearth
d   had it buried in the Dead Sea

773. **Ebed-melech the Ethiopian lowered old cast clouts and rags by cords to Jeremiah in the dungeon where he had been put by the princes, because, while hauling Jeremiah out of the dungeon, Ebed-melech wished**
[Jeremiah 38:6–13]
a   to cover Jeremiah's nakedness
b   to prevent injury to Jeremiah
c   to make Jeremiah appear ridiculous
d   Jeremiah to clean the sides of the dungeon

774. **King Zedekiah was reluctant to surrender to the Babylonians (as the Lord, through Jeremiah, urged him to do), because he** [Jeremiah 38:17–19]
a   did not trust Nebuchadrezzar
b   still thought he could hold out in Jerusalem
c   doubted that he could stand the rigors of the Babylonian climate
d   feared the Jews already in the hands of the Chaldeans

775. **When the Babylonians overran Jerusalem and captured Jeremiah, they** [Jeremiah 39:11–18; 40:1–6]
a   let him go
b   slew him
c   took him to Babylon
d   handed him over to the Jews who were already with the Chaldeans

776. **When Gedaliah, appointed by the King of Babylon governor of those Jews not taken to exile in Babylon, refused to allow Johanan to slay Ishmael, he showed**
[Jeremiah 40:5, 13–16; 41:1–3]
a   humanity but poor judgment
b   cowardice but good judgment
c   generosity and good judgment
d   political sophistication

777. **In the event, Johanan** [Jeremiah 41:11–15]
a   did kill Ishmael
b   did not kill Ishmael

    c may or may not have killed Ishmael
    d was killed by Ishmael

778. **When Jeremiah asked the Lord, on behalf of the non-exiled Jews, what they should do next, the reply came through in ten**   [Jeremiah 42:1–7]
    a minutes
    b hours
    c days
    d weeks

779. **The Lord told the nonexiles (through Jeremiah) to**
                                    [Jeremiah 42:8–17]
    a stay where they were
    b go to Egypt
    c go to Babylon
    d become nomads

780. **The nonexiles, in turn, declared to Jeremiah their conviction that**   [Jeremiah 43:2–3]
    a he spoke for the Lord, and the Lord's advice was good
    b he spoke for the Lord, but the Lord's advice was bad
    c he did not speak for the Lord, but the advice was good
    d he did not speak for the Lord, and the advice was bad

781. **To give a sign to the people of Judah that He would punish them for going into Egypt against His express command, the Lord declared that He would give**
                                    [Jeremiah 44:29–30]
    a them into the hand of Pharaoh-hophra, King of Egypt
    b Pharaoh-hophra into the hand of his enemies
    c Nebuchadrezzar of Babylon into the hand of Pharaoh-hophra
    d Jeremiah into the hand of Pharaoh-hophra

782. **"Fear, and the pit, and the snare, shall be upon thee," said the Lord, to be experienced**   [Jeremiah 48:43–44]
    a simultaneously
    b successively
    c in reverse order
    d after a long delay

783. **"I have laid a snare for thee," said the Lord, "and thou art also taken, O**   [Jeremiah 50:24]
    a Assyria"
    b Babylon"
    c Israel"
    d Judah"

784. **The one nation specified by the Lord to be a destroyer of Babylon was**   [Jeremiah 51:11, 28]
    a Assyria
    b Media

    c Parthia
    d Persia

785. **Nebuchadrezzar "hath devoured me . . . he hath made
me an empty vessel, he hath swallowed me up like a
dragon, he hath filled his belly with my delicates, he hath
cast me out,"**   [Jeremiah 51:34–35; 50:1]
    a the inhabitant of Zion said
    b the Lord said, shall the inhabitant of Zion say
    c Jeremiah said, the Lord said, shall the inhabitant of
       Zion say
    d Jeremiah said

Lamentations
of Jeremiah

786. **Do unto my enemies, Jerusalem beseeches the Lord,**
                                [Lamentations 1:22]
    a as I would have them do unto me
    b as Thou hast done unto me
    c as they would do unto me
    d as I have done unto Thee

787. **Children and sucklings in Jerusalem**
                           [Lamentations 2:11, 19]
    a are sheltered from harm
    b work for their food
    c swoon in the streets
    d are disowned by their parents

788. **Their offspring the women of Jerusalem, Lamentations
implies,**   [Lamentations 2:20; 4:10]
    a eat
    b sell into slavery
    c work to death
    d sacrifice to the Lord

789. **Lamentations 3 speaks of "the wormwood and the**
                               [Lamentations 3:19]
    a oil"
    b sage"
    c gall"
    d bile"

790. **"He putteth his mouth in the dust; if so be**
                              [Lamentations 3:29]
   a   there is no hope"
   b   there may be hope"
   c   there is always hope"
   d   there is never hope"

791. **"Like the ostriches in the wilderness," the "daughter of my people is become**   [Lamentations 4:3]
   a   panic-stricken"
   b   hungry"
   c   senseless"
   d   cruel"

792. **Lamentations 5 does not say that**
                         [Lamentations 5:11, 12; 4:10]
   a   women are ravished in Zion
   b   maids are ravished in the cities of Judah
   c   pitiful women have sodden their own children
   d   princes are hanged up by their hand

Ezekiel

793. **The word of the Lord came to Ezekiel, in exile in the land of the Chaldeans, through a great cloud and a fire unfolding itself, from the midst of which came the likeness of four living creatures, each with** [Ezekiel 1:1–6]
   a   two faces and two wings
   b   two faces and four wings
   c   four faces and two wings
   d   four faces and four wings

794. **The faces of these creatures, according to Ezekiel 1, included those of**   [Ezekiel 1:10]
   a   an ox
   b   an ostrich
   c   an ass
   d   a tiger

795. **The four wheels upon the earth by the living creatures "had one likeness: and their appearance . . . was as it were**   [Ezekiel 1:15–16]
   a   a square within a circle"
   b   two ears within two eyes"
   c   a wheel in the middle of a wheel"
   d   fire within ice"

796. **Over the heads of these creatures there was a**
                                            [Ezekiel 1:22, 25]
    a   pillar of fire
    b   column of smoke
    c   thick fog
    d   firmament

797. **Ezekiel received from the Lord a** [Ezekiel 2:9–10; 1:28]
    a   rod and staff
    b   roll of a book
    c   stone tablet
    d   portion of manna

798. **As commanded, that which he had received from the Lord Ezekiel**   [Ezekiel 3:1–3]
    a   ate
    b   carried
    c   perused
    d   split

799. **Thereupon Ezekiel was, by the Spirit,** [Ezekiel 3:12–14]
    a   flattened
    b   bowed over
    c   pushed
    d   lifted up

800. **Ezekiel was commanded by the Lord to lie, bound, upon his left side for**   [Ezekiel 4:4–5, 8]
    a   3 days
    b   39 days
    c   390 days
    d   3,900 days

801. **And on his right side Ezekiel was commanded to lie, bound, for**   [Ezekiel 4:6, 8]
    a   4 days
    b   40 days
    c   400 days
    d   4,000 days

802. **The daily ration of meat that the Lord allowed Ezekiel while he lay upon his side was apparently about**
                     [Ezekiel 4:10; Davis, *Dictionary*, p. 811]
    a   ¼ pound
    b   ¾ pound
    c   1½ pounds
    d   2 pounds

803. **And Ezekiel's water ration was a little less than**
                                                [Ezekiel 4:11]
    a   ¼ quart
    b   1 quart
    c   2 quarts
    d   3 quarts

804. **Said the Lord, "Let not the**   [Ezekiel 7:12]
    a buyer rejoice, nor the seller mourn"
    b seller rejoice, nor the buyer mourn"
    c buyer and seller rejoice"
    d buyer and seller mourn"

805. **Ezekiel was taken by a lock of his head and lifted up between heaven and earth as he**   [Ezekiel 8:1-3]
    a sat in his house
    b walked in the fields
    c was trimming his hair
    d was swimming

806. **The man clothed in linen, who had a writer's inkhorn by his side, was directed to put a mark upon the foreheads of those in Jerusalem who were**   [Ezekiel 9:1-6]
    a to be slaughtered by the executioners
    b to be spared by the executioners
    c to be the executioners
    d in turn to slay the executioners

807. **The dynamic peculiarity of the wheels, mentioned again in Ezekiel 10 (see No. 795), was that they**
                                         [Ezekiel 10:10-11]
    a rotated backward as they went forward
    b rotated forward as they went backward
    c moved without rotating
    d rotated without moving

808. **At the Lord's command, Ezekiel left as one who goes forth into captivity, by**   [Ezekiel 12:1-7]
    a fastening himself behind a cart
    b digging through the wall with his hands
    c taking no more than he could carry on his head
    d crawling on hands and knees to the city gate

809. **The Lord was determined that the proverb about the land of Israel that went, "The days are prolonged, and every vision faileth," should be**   [Ezekiel 12:21-23]
    a respected
    b interpreted
    c put an end to
    d voted on

810. **The three men named by the Lord as ones He would spare (but not their children) were they in the faithless land were**   [Ezekiel 14:12-20]
    a Noah, Abraham, Job
    b Abraham, Jacob, David
    c Jacob, David, Solomon
    d Noah, Daniel, Job

811. **The inhabitants of Jerusalem were likened by the Lord to the wood of the vine because that wood**
                                         [Ezekiel 15:1-8]

    a   grows slowly
    b   is good only for fuel
    c   is the source of intemperance
    d   decays rapidly

812. **Jerusalem, says the Lord, played the whore with a difference: she**   [Ezekiel 16:30–34]
    a   demanded unconscionable sums
    b   demanded nothing, gave nothing
    c   demanded nothing, gave gifts
    d   both demanded hire and gave it

813. **"As is the mother, so is her daughter," was a proverb foreseen by the Lord, applicable to Jerusalem, one which He indicated would be**   [Ezekiel 16:43–45]
    a   appreciative
    b   stimulating
    c   inaccurate
    d   pejorative

814. **The Lord God compared Jerusalem with Sodom**
                               [Ezekiel 16:46–50]
    a   favorably
    b   unfavorably
    c   indifferently
    d   indecisively

815. **As to forgiveness of Jerusalem, that, said the Lord, was**
                        [Ezekiel 16:53, 55, 60–63]
    a   unthinkable
    b   barely possible
    c   uncertain
    d   assured

816. **The Lord tells Ezekiel (see No. 764) that the old proverb concerning the land of Israel, that "The fathers have eaten sour grapes, and the children's teeth are set on edge," is**   [Ezekiel 18:1–20]
    a   acceptable
    b   unacceptable
    c   acceptable for heinous offenses
    d   applicable to non-Israelites

817. **To lend at interest was, in the Lord's eyes, to commit**
                           [Ezekiel 18:8, 13, 17]
    a   an unrighteous act
    b   a righteous act
    c   an act morally neutral
    d   an act fraught with risk

818. **Suppose that man A acts righteously for a long time and then acts wickedly for a short period before his death, while man B is wicked for many years, but then turns righteous for a short period: in Ezekiel the Lord evidently implied that**   [Ezekiel 18:21–24; 33:10–20]

    a both shall die
    b neither shall die
    c A shall die, not B
    d B shall die, not A

819. **The sins that the Lord charged the princes of Israel with (in Ezekiel 22) did not include** [Ezekiel 22:6–12]
    a humbling their sisters
    b lewdly defiling their daughters-in-law
    c committing abomination with their mothers
    d discovering the nakedness of their fathers

820. **The two sisters who "committed whoredoms in Egypt," where "there were their breasts pressed, and there they bruised the teats of their virginity," were named** [Ezekiel 23:2–4]
    a Ahaloh and Ahaliboh
    b Ahaboh and Ahaliloh
    c Aholah and Aholibah
    d Ahoboh and Ahalilah

821. **The sister of whom the Lord said that "in her youth . . . [the chosen men of Assyria] lay with her and . . . bruised the breasts of her virginity, and poured their whoredom upon her" was the one representing** [Ezekiel 23:4–8]
    a Alexandria
    b Babylon
    c Jerusalem
    d Samaria

822. **The other sister, while in Egypt, had "doted upon their paramours" there, whose "flesh is as the flesh of** [Ezekiel 23:11, 19–20]
    a asses"
    b horses"
    c lions"
    d swans"

823. **(Continuing No. 822) "and whose issue is like the issue of** [Ezekiel 23:20]
    a asses"
    b horses"
    c lions"
    d swans"

824. **"Bind the tire of thine head upon thee, and put on thy shoes upon thy feet, and cover not thy lips," commanded the Lord of Ezekiel, for Ezekiel's wife was about to** [Ezekiel 24:15–18]
    a bear a child
    b commit adultery
    c blaspheme the Lord
    d die

825. **"I will also scrape her dust from her, and make her like the top of a rock," said the Lord of** [Ezekiel 26:4]
    a Babylon
    b Edom
    c Moab
    d Tyre

826. **The city of Tyrus did not provide a market for**
                                    [Ezekiel 27:3, 12, 13, 17, 22]
    a silver, iron, tin and lead from Tarshish
    b persons of men and vessels of brass from Arabia
    c wheat, honey, oil and balm from Judah
    d spices, precious stones, and gold from Sheba

827. **"Thine heart was lifted up because of thy beauty; thou hast corrupted thy wisdom by reason of thy brightness," said the Lord, of** [Ezekiel 28:1, 12, 17]
    a the King of Tyre
    b Sidon
    c Pharaoh, King of Egypt
    d Ezekiel

828. **"I will cause the fish of thy rivers to stick unto thy scales," said the Lord, to Pharaoh (through Ezekiel), meaning that Pharaoh would be** [Ezekiel 29:1, 2–5]
    a encumbered with fish
    b unable to sell his fish
    c unwilling to eat his fish
    d without usable scales

829. **The Lord decided to give the land of Egypt to Nebuchadrezzar because he** [Ezekiel 29:18–20]
    a got nothing out of the conquest of Tyre
    b was *persona non grata* to Pharaoh
    c foresaw that it would be only a desert
    d listened to Ezekiel

830. **The Lord said Ezekiel was, to the children of his people, "as a very lovely song of one that hath a pleasant voice, and can play well on an instrument," since his audience**
                                              [Ezekiel 33:31–32]
    a was so captivated that they followed his suggestion
    b heard his words but did not follow them
    c demanded so much of him he was left exhausted
    d consisted almost entirely of women

831. **"In the fire of my jealousy have I spoken," said**
                                                  [Ezekiel 36:5]
    a the Lord
    b Ezekiel
    c Nebuchadrezzar
    d Pharaoh

832. **Ezekiel, set down in the midst of a valley full of bones, was asked, "Son of man, can these bones live?" and he answered, "O Lord God,** [Ezekiel 37:1–3]

a   certainly not"
b   if they are the bones of man"
c   not without thy spirit"
d   thou knowest"

833. "And as I prophesied," said Ezekiel, "there was a noise, and, behold, a shaking, and the bones   [Ezekiel 37:7]
a   danced"
b   rolled over the cliff's edge"
c   fought"
d   came together"

834. Gog and Magog were, respectively,   [Ezekiel 38:2-3]
a   idol and people
b   ruler and people
c   people and ruler
d   people and idol

835. When the forces of the chief prince of Meshech and Tubal have been destroyed, said the Lord, the Israelites will turn their enemy's weapons into
[Ezekiel 39:1-5, 9-10]
a   fuel
b   plowshares
c   exports
d   museum pieces

836. Ezekiel, obeying the command of the man with a line of flax and a measuring reed, must be credited with great
[Ezekiel 40:3-49; 41-48]
a   courage
b   retentiveness
c   sympathy
d   caution

837. The Levitical priests, the sons of Zadok, when ministering at the gates of the inner court, and within, are not to gird themselves (declared the Lord) with anything that
[Ezekiel 44:15-18]
a   is transparent
b   is colored
c   causes sweat
d   is cumbersome

838. The hair of these priests' heads was to be
[Ezekiel 44:15, 20]
a   shaven
b   polled
c   let grow into long locks
d   curled

839. These priests could marry   [Ezekiel 44:15, 22]
a   not at all
b   virgins

    c   only widows
    d   divorced women

840. **The circumference of the city as planned by the Lord
      was to be about**   [Ezekiel 48:35]
    a   1 mile
    b   5 miles
    c   11 miles
    d   23 miles

Daniel

841. **Belteshazzar was of the**   [Daniel 1:3, 7]
    a   Babylonian nobility
    b   Babylonian commonalty
    c   Israelite nobility
    d   Israelite commonalty

842. **For ten days Daniel was given only water to drink and
      pulse to eat,**   [Daniel 1:11-14]
    a   for prophesying against Nebuchadnezzar
    b   for assaulting his companions in exile, Hananiah,
        Mishael, and Azariah
    c   because he was indisposed
    d   at his own request

843. **Compared with the task faced by Joseph with respect
      to Pharaoh's dreams, that faced by Daniel with respect
      to Nebuchadnezzar's dreams was**
                     [Daniel 2:1-16; Genesis 41:8]
    a   less difficult
    b   more difficult
    c   of about the same degree of difficulty
    d   noncomparable in difficulty

844. **The appeal by Daniel and his companions to the Lord
      for information that would avert the threatened destruc-
      tion of all the wise men of Babylon was**
                     [Daniel 2:13-19]
    a   an example of pure altruism
    b   motivated by a love of learning
    c   tinged with self-interest
    d   a skeptical trial of the Lord's powers

845. **The terrible, bright, great image that stood before Ne-
      buchadnezzar in his dream, with head of gold, breast**

and arms of silver, belly and thighs of brass and legs of
iron, had feet of   [Daniel 2:31–33]
a clay
b putty
c iron and clay
d iron and putty

846. Daniel's interpretation of Nebuchadnezzar's dream was,
to the King personally,   [Daniel 2:36–46]
a terrifying
b banal
c chaotic
d gratifying

847. When the most mighty men of Nebuchadnezzar's army
bound Shadrach, Meshach and Abednego and cast them
into the burning fiery furnace heated seven times more
than its wonted level, the flames consumed
[Daniel 3:19–27]
a Shadrach, but not Abednego or Meshach
b Meshach, but not Abednego or Shadrach
c Abednego, but not Meshach or Shadrach
d the most mighty men

848. Being about to interpret to Nebuchadnezzar the dream
in which that King was represented by a great tree
visible to all the earth, Daniel experienced a feeling of
[Daniel 4:9–11, 19]
a anticipation
b pride
c feebleness
d danger

849. Nebuchadnezzar was driven from among men but did
not   [Daniel 4:33]
a eat grass as oxen
b have his hairs grow like eagles' feathers
c have his nails become like birds' claws
d climb trees like an ape

850. Belshazzar was Nebuchadnezzar's   [Daniel 5:2]
a son
b nephew
c uncle
d cousin

851. The moving finger wrote on a wall of   [Daniel 5:5]
a stone
b plaster
c brick
d papyrus

852. "MĒNE, MĒNE, TĒKEL, U-PHĀRSIN," was inter-
preted by Daniel to mean   [Daniel 5:25–28]
a led, led, taken, died

    b   mine, mine, yours, theirs
    c   numbered, numbered, weighed, divided
    d   warning, warning, flee, escape

853. **According to the law of the Medes and the Persians, no
      decree or statute established by the King**
                                                      [Daniel 6:8, 15]
    a   was valid without a termination date
    b   applied to the King or his household
    c   was published
    d   could be changed

854. **King Darius, having cast Daniel into the lions' den,**
                                                      [Daniel 6:16]
    a   expressed a hope that he would be saved
    b   remarked that he was getting his just deserts
    c   lay a wager on the lions
    d   indicated no preference as to the outcome

855. **As it turned out,**   [Daniel 6:22]
    a   Daniel slew the lions
    b   the lions ate Daniel
    c   it was a hard-fought draw
    d   the lions let Daniel alone

856. **To the question, "How long shall it be to the end of
      these wonders?" the man clothed in linen replied,**
                                                      [Daniel 12:6–7]
    a   "for a time, times, and an half"
    b   "for an half, a time, and times"
    c   "for times, a time, and an half"
    d   "for a time, an half, and two times"

Hosea

857. **Hosea the prophet lived in the time of**   [Hosea 1:1]
    a   Moses
    b   Uzziah
    c   Belshazzar
    d   Belteshazzar

858. **The Lord commanded Hosea to take a "wife of whore-
      doms," because**   [Hosea 1:2]
    a   Hosea had sinned
    b   the whore had sinned
    c   the people had sinned
    d   no one had sinned

859. **Hosea's third child by Gomer was, by order of the Lord, named Loammi, to indicate that they were not**
                                                    [Hosea 1:3–9]
      a   pitied
      b   forgiven
      c   God's people
      d   avenged

860. **The Lord then commanded Hosea to love**   [Hosea 3:1]
      a   Gomer's sister
      b   a foreign princess
      c   a temple virgin
      d   an adulteress

861. **"Wine, and new wine," says Hosea 4,**   [Hosea 4:11]
      a   "magnify the spirit"
      b   "do honor to the Lord"
      c   "take away the heart"
      d   "propitiate the intruder"

862. **"Your goodness," as Hosea says of Judah, "is as**
                                                    [Hosea 6:4]
      a   the setting sun"
      b   the evening star"
      c   the crescent moon"
      d   a morning cloud"

863. **"For they have sown the wind," says Hosea 8, "and they shall reap the**   [Hosea 8:7]
      a   harvest"
      b   whirlwind"
      c   rain"
      d   wind"

864. **"Give them, O Lord:" says Hosea, of Ephraim, "what wilt thou give? give them**   [Hosea 9:14, 1, 6, 8]
      a   a reward upon every cornfloor"
      b   a snare of a fowler"
      c   a miscarrying womb and dry breasts"
      d   nettles in their pleasant places for their silver and thorns in their tabernacles"

865. **"Ye have plowed wickedness," says Hosea, "ye have reaped**   [Hosea 10:13]
      a   virtue"
      b   evil"
      c   iniquity"
      d   equity"

866. **"Ephraim feedeth on wind, and**   [Hosea 12:1]
      a   reapeth the whirlwind"
      b   endureth the rain"
      c   gathers the rain"
      d   followeth after the east wind"

867. **In Samaria "their infants shall be dashed in pieces" and "their women with child shall be ripped up" because**
[Hosea 13:16]
   a   Samaria is attempting to grow too large
   b   they will otherwise spread leprosy
   c   Samaria has rebelled against her God
   d   blind fate decrees it

Joel

868. **The plague of locusts described in Joel does not include**
[Joel 1:4]
   a   palmerworms
   b   galleyworms
   c   cankerworms
   d   caterpillars

869. **Joel declared, beat your**   [Joel 3:10]
   a   plowshares into swords, your pruninghooks into spears
   b   swords into plowshares, your spears into pruninghooks
   c   pruninghooks into swords, your plowshares into spears
   d   swords into pruninghooks, your spears into plowshares

Amos

870. **Amos lived**   [Amos 1:1; Hosea 1:1]
   a   about the same time as Hosea
   b   well before Hosea
   c   well after Hosea
   d   either before or after Hosea, which, is not known

871. **It will be "to profane my holy name," said the Lord, when**
[Amos 2:7]
   a   they sell the poor for a pair of shoes

b they pant after the dust of the earth on the head
   of the poor
c a man and his father go in unto the same maid
d in the house of their god they drink the wine of the
   condemned

872. "As the shepherd taketh out of the mouth of the lion
      two legs, or a piece of an ear," said the Lord, so shall
      rescue be effected for those in   [Amos 3:12]
      a Jerusalem
      b Babylon
      c Bozrah
      d Samaria

873. "Prepare to meet thy God," said the Lord, using "meet"
      in the sense of   [Amos 4:12]
      a greet
      b encounter
      c cross paths
      d keep an appointment

874. It is "as if a man did flee from a lion, and a bear met
      him; or went into the house, and leaned his hand on
      the wall, and a serpent bit him," with those who
                                                [Amos 5:18–19]
      a desire the day of the Lord
      b put their trust in the Baals
      c depend on Egypt
      d drown their sorrows in wine

875. In Amos 6, those who "invent to themselves instruments
      of musick, like David," are the object of the Lord's
                                                [Amos 6:1, 5, 7]
      a approbation
      b commiseration
      c indignation
      d exultation

876. Amos the prophet was a   [Amos 7:14]
      a herdman
      b priest
      c fisherman
      d small businessman

Obadiah

877. The land for which Obadiah prophesied destruction was
      that given originally to
                        [Obadiah 1, 8, 10, 18; Genesis 25: 29–33]

a   Jacob
b   Esau
c   Joseph
d   Benjamin

Jonah

878. **The Lord ordered Jonah to go to a city located**
                                                      [Jonah 1:1–2]
      a   on the seacoast
      b   inland
      c   on an island
      d   on a mountain top

879. **When the Lord sent out a great wind into the sea, so
      that the ship threatened to break up, Jonah was found**
                                                      [Jonah 1:4–5]
      a   clinging to the foremast
      b   sick at the ship's rail
      c   eating a hearty meal
      d   fast asleep

880. **The sailors' notion of the source of the trouble was**
                                                      [Jonah 1:7, 10]
      a   fantastically inaccurate
      b   understandably in error
      c   more correct than incorrect
      d   absolutely correct

881. **Jonah was cast into the sea**   [Jonah 1:12]
      a   at his own request
      b   without his expressing an opinion on it
      c   while slightly demurring
      d   over his violent objection

882. **Jonah was in the belly of the great fish for**
                                                      [Jonah 1:17]
      a   three days and nights
      b   seven days and nights
      c   thirteen days and nights
      d   forty days and nights

833. **The fish vomited out Jonah upon the dry land because**
                                                      [Jonah 2:10]
      a   Jonah irritated it
      b   Jonah persuaded it
      c   the sailors harpooned it
      d   the Lord spoke to it

884. **After Jonah prophesied the destruction of Nineveh to its inhabitants, he found himself unhappy because they had**   [Jonah 3:4–10; 4:1–4]
   a paid him no heed
   b asked him too many questions
   c threw him into a lion's den
   d responded all too well

885. **The worm's killing of the gourd that shaded Jonah on the outskirts of Nineveh was designed by the Lord to give Jonah**   [Jonah 4:6–10]
   a something to do
   b a sense of proportion
   c a sense of humor
   d reassurance

Micah

886. **"Declare ye it not at**   [Micah 1:10]
   a Aphrah"
   b Gath"
   c Saphir"
   d Zaanan"

887. **The peoples between whom the Lord shall judge shall beat their**   [Micah 4:3]
   a swords into plowshares
   b plowshares into swords
   c spears into plowshares
   d pruninghooks into swords

888. **A Messianic passage in Micah denotes as the origin of the future ruler in Israel**   [Micah 5:2]
   a Jerusalem
   b Bethlehem Ephratah
   c Sardanapalus
   d Gath

889. **Micah asserts that all the Lord requires is that His people**   [Micah 6:6–8]
   a supply thousands of rams for burnt offerings
   b donate ten thousands of rivers of oil
   c give their firstborn for their transgressions
   d do justly, love mercy, and walk humbly with God

890. **False weights and measures are, in Micah,**
                                           [Micah 6:10–11]
   a   not referred to
   b   mentioned in passing
   c   emphatically condemned
   d   condoned

Nahum

891. **Nahum prophesied the overthrow of**   [Nahum 1:1]
   a   Babylon
   b   Jerusalem
   c   Tyre
   d   Nineveh

892. **I "will discover thy skirts upon thy face, and I will shew the nations thy nakedness, and the kingdoms thy shame," said**   [Nahum 3:5]
   a   Sargon
   b   Nahum
   c   the Lord
   d   Lodebar

Habakkuk

893. **"That bitter and hasty nation," so termed by the Lord, was the**   [Habakkuk 1:6]
   a   Assyrians
   b   Israelites
   c   Chaldeans
   d   Egyptians

894. **The proud man, who "enlargeth his desire as hell, and is as death," also**   [Habakkuk 2:5]
   a   "cannot be satisfied"
   b   "is always with us"
   c   "sows sorrow and suffering"
   d   "demands more than he gives"

Zephaniah

895. Zephaniah was a descendant of   [Zephaniah 1:1]
a Habakkuk
b Nahum
c Micah
d Hizkiah

896. The Lord declared He will punish those who say in their heart that the Lord will do   [Zephaniah 1:12]
a neither good nor evil
b good, but not evil
c evil, but not good
d both good and evil

897. "I will bring distress upon men," said the Lord, "because they have sinned against the Lord: and their blood shall be poured out as   [Zephaniah 1:17]
a water"
b dust"
c wine"
d pitch"

898. Not listed for destruction by the Lord in Zephaniah 2 is   [Zephaniah 2:1-15]

a Assyria
b Babylon
c Ethiopia
d Nineveh

Haggai

899. You will have noticed, said the Lord, through the Prophet Haggai, that "he that earneth wages, earneth wages to put it into a bag with holes," and the cause for this is   [Haggai 1:3-6, 9]
a inflation
b tribute levied by Darius
c your delay in rebuilding my house
d the extortionate practices of the money lenders of Judah

Zechariah

900. **The word of the Lord came to the Prophets Haggai and Zechariah**   [Zechariah 1:1; Haggai 1:1]
  a   simultaneously
  b   in that order
  c   in the reverse order
  d   in what order, it is not known

901. **The Lord reveals to Zechariah that He is "sore displeased" with "the heathen that are at ease" because, seeing His anger at Jerusalem, they had**
                        [Zechariah 1:15–16]
  a   overreacted
  b   underreacted
  c   reacted in the wrong direction
  d   not reacted at all

902. **Zechariah reports that, "I turned, and lifted up mine eyes, and looked, and behold a flying**
                        [Zechariah 5:1]
  a   object"
  b   horse"
  c   lamp"
  d   roll"

903. **The streets of Jerusalem, said the Lord to Zechariah, will be full of**   [Zechariah 8:4–5]
  a   shops and market places with true measures and balances
  b   boys and girls playing
  c   priests praying
  d   peoples from all nations

904. **"The idols," says Zechariah 10, "have spoken**
                        [Zechariah 10:2]
  a   vanity"
  b   lies"
  c   nothing"
  d   truths"

905. **When Zechariah broke the staff he had named Beauty (the other one being named Bands), he thereby annulled**
                        [Zechariah 11:7–14]
  a   the brotherhood between Judah and Israel
  b   the covenant he had made with all the people
  c   the understanding with Darius
  d   his own power as a prophet

906. **The Lord's word concerning the future of Israel (in Zechariah 12) showed a preference on His part for**
                                        [Zechariah 12:7]
    a   the tents of Judah
    b   the house of David
    c   the inhabitants of Jerusalem
    d   none of these three

907. **The Lord indicated that He would change the topography of the land around Jerusalem, in that day when He defeated her enemies, making it**
                                    [Zechariah 14:1–4, 10]
    a   flatter
    b   more mountainous
    c   more swampy
    d   more hilly

Malachi

908. **The Lord expressed discontent at being offered in sacrifice animals**   [Malachi 1:8]
    a   other than rams, bulls, or goats
    b   blind, lame, or sick
    c   imported from other lands
    d   sacrificed also to the Baals

909. **The Lord expressed His attitude toward divorce as one of**   [Malachi 2:16]
    a   hatred
    b   scorn
    c   tolerance
    d   acceptance

St. Matthew

910. **The descent of Joseph, the husband of Mary the mother of Jesus, was from Jacob through**   [Matthew 1:1–3]
    a   Reuben
    b   Judas

      c Joseph
      d Dan

911. **In the gospel according to Matthew, the number of
generations between Abraham (the father of Isaac) and
Jesus was**   [Matthew 1:2–16]
      a 17
      b 28
      c 39
      d 42

912. **When Joseph learned that his espoused, Mary, was with
child, his first inclination (before an angel of the Lord
visited him in a dream) was to**   [Matthew 1:18–20]
      a act as if he were the father-to-be
      b denounce her to the priests
      c put her away without public exposure
      d send her abroad

913. **The angel of the Lord instructed Joseph to call Mary's
son Jesus, for He was to**   [Matthew 1:21]
      a restore Jerusalem
      b transmit messages from the Lord
      c save His people from their sins
      d preach love, not hate

914. **Jesus was born in**   [Matthew 2:1]
      a Bethlehem of Judaea
      b Bethlehem of Zebulun
      c Nazareth
      d Jerusalem

915. **The wise men, because they saw in the East the star of
Him who had been born King of the Jews, came to**
                        [Matthew 2:1–2]
      a Jerusalem
      b Bethlehem
      c Nazareth
      d Capernaum

916. **The source of Herod's information as to the town where
the Christ was to be born was**
                [Matthew 2:1–8; Micah 5:2]
      a the wise men
      b his security police
      c Micah
      d Joseph

917. **In Matthew, the number of wise men is**
                      [Matthew 2:1–12]
      a two
      b three
      c four
      d unspecified

918. **Joseph's flight with Jesus and Mary to Egypt, just before Herod ordered the slaughter in Bethlehem and its vicinity, also served to** [Matthew 2:13–15; Hosea 11:1]
   a prove the power of the Lord
   b alert Israel to the menace it faced
   c fulfill a prophecy in Hosea
   d reveal that the Lord's anger at the Pharaohs had cooled

919. **Herod's reaction to the wise men was to order the slaughter, in Bethlehem and its vicinity, of certain** [Matthew 2:16]
   a wise men
   b parents named either Mary or Joseph
   c children
   d Jews

920. **When Joseph, returning with his family to Israel, selected Nazareth, this choice served to** [Matthew 2:19–23]
   a erase his unpleasant memories of Bethlehem
   b place him close to the border
   c put him in touch with influential friends
   d fulfill what had been spoken by the prophets

921. **John the Baptist, preaching in the wilderness of Judaea, wore a garment of** [Matthew 3:1, 4]
   a goatskin
   b camel's hair
   c papyrus
   d wool

922. **John the Baptist's food was** [Matthew 3:4]
   a locusts and wild honey
   b wild honey and manna
   c locusts and manna
   d manna and troglodytes

923. **When Jesus came from Galilee to the Jordan to be baptized by John, John was** [Matthew 3:13–14]
   a overly persuasive
   b ready
   c reluctant
   d despondent

924. **Upon Jesus' baptism, when the voice from heaven said, "This is my beloved son," the Spirit of God descended like** [Matthew 3:16–17]
   a an eagle
   b a cloud
   c a dove
   d a pillar of fire

925. **Jesus was then led up into the wilderness by** [Matthew 4:1]
   a the Spirit of God

   b   the devil
   c   John the Baptist
   d   no one

926. **Jesus' utterance, that "It is written, Man shall not live by bread alone," was occasioned by the devil's**
                                              [Matthew 4:3–4]
   a   assertion to the contrary
   b   suggestion that Jesus turn stones to bread
   c   offer of bread to Jesus
   d   threat to deprive Israel of food

927. **To the devil's urging that He prove Himself the Son of God by casting Himself down from the pinnacle of the temple, Jesus replied that**   [Matthew 4:5–7]
   a   no pinnacle was high enough to test God's power
   b   casting the devil down would be a better proof
   c   it is written, "Thou shalt not tempt the Lord thy God"
   d   a courageous devil would himself cast Jesus down

928. **Jesus left Nazareth and went to dwell in Capernaum, when He**   [Matthew 4:12–13]
   a   was reminded of the prophecy by Esaias (Isaiah)
   b   was dared by the devil to do so
   c   thought He should be on the shores of Galilee
   d   heard that John had been cast into prison

929. **James and John joined Jesus as disciples**
                                              [Matthew 4:21–22]
   a   when Jesus called them
   b   as soon as they saw Him
   c   because their father, Zebedee, told them to
   d   at the insistence of the first two disciples, Simon (called Peter) and Andrew his brother

930. **In the Sermon on the Mount, Jesus taught that**
                                              [Matthew 5:1–11]
   a   "Blessed are the meek, for they shall see God"
   b   "Blessed are the merciful, for they shall be called the children of God"
   c   "Blessed are the poor in spirit, for they shall inherit the earth"
   d   "Blessed are they which are persecuted for righteousness' sake: for their's is the kingdom of heaven"

931. **"Ye are the salt of the earth," said Jesus to the disciples, warning against**   [Matthew 5:13]
   a   offering themselves too freely
   b   losing their savour
   c   affecting sweetness
   d   charging for their services

932. **"Ye are the light of the world," said Jesus to the disciples, warning against**   [Matthew 5:14–16]

    a blinding others by overpowering display
    b believing that others too have light
    c hiding their light under a bushel
    d assuming that all others will agree

933. **Jesus instructed unqualifiedly against observance of the following rule from the Old Testament:**
[Matthew 5:21–42]
    a "Thou shalt not kill; and whosoever shall kill shall be in danger of the judgment"
    b "Thou shalt not commit adultery"
    c "Whosoever shall put away his wife, let him give her a writing of divorcement"
    d "An eye for an eye, and a tooth for a tooth"

934. **The specific warning of punishment by hell fire is first encountered in the Bible when Jesus warns that one should not** [Matthew 5:22]
    a say, "Thou fool"
    b look at a woman lustfully
    c say more than simply "yes" or "no"
    d refuse him who would borrow

935. **"If thy right eye offend thee, pluck it out and cast it from thee," said Jesus, immediately following his admonition against** [Matthew 5:27–29]
    a committing adultery in one's heart
    b the old saying, "An eye for an eye and a tooth for a tooth"
    c swearing at all
    d growing angry at one's brother

936. **You are doing no more than do publicans (tax farmers, or alternatively, tax collectors), observed Jesus, if you**
[Matthew 5:46]
    a salute only your superiors
    b love those who love you
    c lend only to those who lend to you
    d give only to beggars

937. **You should not let your left hand know what your right hand is doing, said Jesus; that is, you should**
[Matthew 6:3–4]
    a try to do but one good deed at a time
    b overcome your baser impulses
    c give alms in secret
    d cut off either hand if it offends you

938. **Jesus gave the Lord's Prayer ("Our Father which art in heaven . . ."), in the Matthew 6 version, as a counter-example against prayers that were too** [Matthew 6:7–13]
    a wordy
    b concise
    c prosy
    d archaic

939. **"Lay not up for yourselves treasures upon earth, where moth and rust doth corrupt, and where** [Matthew 6:19]
   a   kings and princes confiscate"
   b   invading armies pillage"
   c   thieves break through and steal"
   d   floods will sweep away"

940. **"No man can serve two masters," said Jesus, because**
                                                   [Matthew 6:24]
   a   if one master loves him the other will hate him
   b   no two masters can cooperate
   c   no day is long enough for double service
   d   he will love one master and hate or despise the other

941. **"Consider the lilies of the field, how they grow; they toil not, neither do they spin," said Jesus, admonishing His listeners not to take thought for** [Matthew 6:28]
   a   food
   b   clothing
   c   housing
   d   transportation

942. **Do not "cast ye your pearls before swine," said Jesus, lest they** [Matthew 7:6]
   a   flee in fear
   b   trample the pearls and turn to attack you
   c   gulp them as common food
   d   exhibit gross indifference

943. **"Ask, and it shall be given you," said Jesus, since you, being evil,** [Matthew 7:7, 9–11]
   a   nevertheless will not give your son a stone when he asks for bread
   b   deny others so much, your Father must compensate for your sins
   c   will sink under your iniquities if you receive no aid
   d   still are good enough to deserve some charity

944. **Jesus' phrase, "for this is the law and the prophets," refers to His admonition to** [Matthew 7:12]
   a   seek first your heavenly Father's kingdom
   b   judge not, that you be not judged
   c   be not anxious about the morrow
   d   do to others as you would have them do to you

945. **"Beware of false prophets," said Jesus, "which come to you in sheep's clothing, but inwardly . . . are ravening** [Matthew 7:15]
   a   leopards"
   b   wolves"
   c   hyenas"
   d   lions"

946. **"Founded upon a rock" and "built . . . upon the sand" in Matthew 7 refer to a** [Matthew 7:24–27]
   a   temple

    b　dam
    c　house
    d　wall

947. Jesus' exclamation, "Verily I say unto you, I have not found so great faith, no, not in Israel," was elicited by the words of the　　　　　　　[Matthew 8:5–10]
    a　leper
    b　centurion
    c　men possessed of demons
    d　Peter's mother-in-law

948. "Let the dead bury their dead," said Jesus, upon
　　　　　　　　　　　　　　　　　[Matthew 8:21–22]
    a　leaving the leper colony after curing those still living
    b　entering Capernaum
    c　hearing a disciple's request for leave to bury his father
    d　learning that the Pharisees refused to hear Him

949. When Jesus had cast the devils into the herd of swine, He was requested by the inhabitants of the nearby city to　　　　　　　[Matthew 8:28–34]
    a　stay and continue
    b　give them His secret
    c　bring back the swine
    d　leave

950. Jesus cured the paralytic ("Arise, take up thy bed, and go unto thine house") because He　　　[Matthew 9:1–8]
    a　had particular sympathy for this man
    b　wanted the scribes to know that He had power to forgive sins
    c　had done the same for the centurion's servant
    d　knew the man would become a disciple

951. Jesus called Matthew to discipleship from a
　　　　　　　　　　　　　　　　　[Matthew 9:9]
    a　money-changing temple
    b　fishing boat
    c　receipt of custom [tax office]
    d　army post

952. When the Pharisees questioned Jesus about the company He kept (Matthew 9), they were questioning His meeting with　　　　　　　[Matthew 9:10–11]
    a　publicans
    b　sinners
    c　publicans and sinners
    d　sinners, including publicans

953. "No man putteth a piece of new cloth unto an old garment," and "Neither do men put new wine into old bottles," since　　　[Matthew 9:16–17; Mark 2:21–22]
    a　the disparity between old and new is displeasing
    b　the gain in quality is not worth the extra cost

    c   the older part will thereby be damaged

    d   the dead hand of tradition prevents such beneficial action

954. **The ruler whose daughter had died, the woman suffering from a hemorrhage of twelve years, and the two blind men, all had in common the fact that they viewed Jesus' powers with**   [Matthew 9:18-29]

    a   skepticism

    b   trust

    c   bewilderment

    d   overoptimism

955. **Say nothing of this event, Jesus expressly admonished the**   [Matthew 9:18-34; 8:5-13]

    a   paralyzed servant

    b   daughter of the ruler

    c   dumb demoniac

    d   two blind men

956. **Jesus gave to His twelve disciples the power to**   [Matthew 10:1]

    a   cast out unclean spirits

    b   calm the winds and the sea

    c   baptize

    d   grant divorces

957. **The twelve apostles included**   [Matthew 10:2-4]

    a   two brothers

    b   two sets of two brothers

    c   three brothers

    d   three sets of two brothers

958. **Of the twelve apostles, as named in Matthew 10, the number that had the same original name as at least one other disciple was**   [Matthew 10:2-4]

    a   none

    b   two

    c   three

    d   four

959. **In Matthew 10, Jesus instructed the apostles to go among the**   [Matthew 10:5-6]

    a   Gentiles

    b   Samaritans

    c   Israelites

    d   Egyptians

960. **Jesus told the apostles to "shake off the dust of your feet" as they**   [Matthew 10:14]

    a   entered a city that received them

    b   entered a house that received them

    c   left a house or city that did not receive them

    d   prepared for the night's rest

961. **Jesus' statement that, although two sparrows are sold for a farthing, yet "one of them shall not fall on the ground without your Father," was followed by His remark that the apostles were of**   [Matthew 10:29-31]

    a no more value than two sparrows

    b less value than one sparrow

    c more value than two sparrows

    d more value than many sparrows

962. **"I came not," said Jesus,**   [Matthew 10:34]

    a "to send peace, but a sword"

    b "to send a sword, but peace"

    c "to enforce peace by the sword"

    d "to send peace or a sword"

963. **The John who queried Jesus from prison, asking, "Art thou he that should come, or do we look for another?" was**   [Matthew 11:2-3; 4:12]

    a John the Baptist

    b John the apostle

    c John Mark

    d John Hyrcanus

964. **"Every . . . house divided against itself shall not stand," declared Jesus, referring to**   [Matthew 12:22-26]

    a Satan

    b the Lord

    c the Israelites

    d the Pharisees

965. **"I say unto you," said Jesus in Matthew 12:36, "in the day of judgment" men "shall give account thereof," with respect to every**   [Matthew 12:36]

    a foolish move they make

    b idle word they speak

    c hateful thought they harbor

    d blasphemy they tolerate

966. **When the man whose unclean spirit has gone out of him returns, after obtaining no rest in walking through dry places, and finds his house empty, swept, and garnished, he then, said Jesus,**   [Matthew 12:43-45]

    a continues upward to a useful, happy life

    b resumes his former deplorable state

    c sinks to lower levels than before

    d seeks an explanation

967. **When Jesus' mother and brethren, standing outside while He was speaking to the people, asked to speak to Him, He**   [Matthew 12:46-50]

    a interrupted His discourse, to hear them

    b rebuked them for interrupting Him

    c implied they stood no closer to Him than His disciples

    d asked them to speak to the people

968. **When Jesus spoke in parables to the great crowd of
      people, He was seated in a**   [Matthew 13:1-3]
      a   ship
      b   chair
      c   cart
      d   hammock

969. **"For whosoever hath, to him shall be given . . . but
      whosoever hath not, from him shall be taken away, even
      that he hath," in Matthew 13, refers to**
                                          [Matthew 13:10-17]
      a   property
      b   friendship
      c   understanding
      d   health

970. **The parable of the pearl of great price tells how**
                                          [Matthew 13:45-46]
      a   it went long unrecognized
      b   it was transferred but through violence
      c   the pearl merchant sold all that he had, to buy it
      d   it increased in value with the passage of time

971. **Jesus' brothers, if "brethren" in this context is taken to
      mean "brothers," were named**   [Matthew 13:55]
      a   James, Peter, Simon and Judas
      b   John, James, Thomas and Judas
      c   James, Matthew, Simon and Peter
      d   James, Joses, Simon and Judas

972. **Matthew 13 speaks of**   [Matthew 13:56]
      a   sisters of Jesus
      b   one sister of Jesus
      c   no sisters of Jesus
      d   a step-sister of Jesus

973. **"A prophet is not without honour, save in his own
      country, and in his own house," said Jesus, referring to**
                                          [Matthew 13:57]
      a   John the Baptist
      b   Himself
      c   His twelve disciples
      d   no one in particular

974. **When Herod's brother's wife's daughter's dance at his
      birthday party pleased him mightily, he rewarded her
      by bringing the head of John the Baptist in a charger**
                                          [Matthew 14:3-11]
      a   on his own initiative
      b   at his wife's request
      c   at the dancer's request
      d   at the request of the guests

975. **When Jesus, hearing of the death of John the Baptist,
      withdrew in a boat "into a desert" and was followed by**

a throng of 5,000 men, besides women and children, he fed them all, although his disciples had only

[Matthew 14:13, 17–21]

a   five loaves and two fishes
b   twenty loaves and forty fishes
c   two loaves and five fishes
d   one loaf and one fish

976. **Jesus walked on the sea because**   [Matthew 14:24–33]
a   it was too rough to launch a boat
b   His boat had been blown far from the shore
c   He desired to restore faith to His disciples
d   He desired to prove His identity to the multitude

977. **Peter walked on the sea**   [Matthew 14:26–29]
a   to proffer aid to Jesus were it needed
b   to demonstrate his discipleship to the multitude
c   to be certain that the One on the water was Jesus, not a spirit
d   because his boat had drifted far from the shore

978. **"O thou of little faith, wherefore didst thou doubt?" said Jesus to**   [Matthew 14:30–31]
a   John
b   Judas
c   Matthew
d   Peter

979. **When the Pharisees and scribes complained to Jesus that His disciples did not wash their hands when they ate bread, He replied that**   [Matthew 15:1–11]
a   their hands were already clean
b   the appeal to tradition was not well grounded
c   a man is defiled not by what goes into his mouth but by what comes out of it
d   the protestors were hypocrites, not themselves observing this rule

980. **"And if the blind lead the blind," said Jesus, "both shall**   [Matthew 15:14]
a   walk in circles"
b   stumble against those with sight"
c   end far from the place they seek"
d   fall into the ditch"

981. **When the Canaanite woman whose daughter was vexed with a devil replied to Jesus, "Truth, Lord: yet the dogs eat of the crumbs which fall from their masters' table," she was referring to**   [Matthew 15:22–28]
a   the disciples
b   herself and her daughter
c   the Israelites
d   mankind

982. **The weather forecasts of the Pharisees and Sadducees included the formula,**   [Matthew 16:1-3]
   a   evening sky red, fair; morning sky red, stormy
   b   evening sky red, stormy; morning sky red, fair
   c   evening or morning sky red, fair
   d   evening or morning sky red, stormy

983. **"Upon this rock I will build my church," and "I will give unto thee the keys of the kingdom of heaven," said Jesus to**   [Matthew 16:17-19]
   a   James the son of Zebedee
   b   John the son of Zebedee
   c   Matthew
   d   Peter

984. **As to the fact that He was Jesus the Christ, Jesus charged His disciples, in Matthew 16, to tell**   [Matthew 16:20]
   a   everyone
   b   no one
   c   all Israelites
   d   no Israelites

985. **"Get thee behind me, Satan," said Jesus to**
                                                    [Matthew 16:23]
   a   Bartholomew
   b   Judas
   c   Peter
   d   Simon the Cananaean

986. **When, after the father of the lunatic had asked Jesus to cure his son, and had told of the efforts he had already made to obtain a cure, Jesus said, "O faithless and perverse generation! how long shall I be with you? how long shall I suffer you?" He was rebuking the**
                                                    [Matthew 17:14-20]
   a   father
   b   son
   c   demon in the son
   d   disciples

987. **When Peter replied to the Capernaum collectors of tribute money that Jesus would pay the tribute, Jesus rebuked him and**   [Matthew 17:24-27]
   a   ordered him to refuse payment
   b   gave him half a shekel to pay under protest
   c   gave him ten shekels to pay
   d   told him to go to the sea and cast for a fish

988. **When the disciples asked Jesus, "who is the greatest in the kingdom of heaven?" He responded indirectly by placing in their midst**   [Matthew 18:1-4]
   a   an ark
   b   an old man
   c   a stone tablet
   d   a child

989. **"If thy brother shall trespass against thee, go and tell him his fault," said Jesus, going first to talk with him** [Matthew 18:15–17]
 a   alone
 b   with one or two witnesses
 c   in the church
 d   as you would with a Gentile or a publican

990. **The parable of the king who wished to settle accounts with his servants was told by Jesus to emphasize His admonition to** [Matthew 18:21–35]
 a   never lend at interest
 b   forgive as you would be forgiven
 c   fulfill contracts as you would have them fulfilled
 d   never borrow from an inferior

991. **When His disciples remarked that branding as adultery the putting away of one's wife (except for fornication) and subsequent marriage with another was a dictum that made it inexpedient to marry, Jesus said that** [Matthew 19:9–12]
 a   only those to whom it is given can receive this saying
 b   if the rule were observed by all, all would find it easier to observe
 c   strengthening of character is never inexpedient
 d   they were too pessimistic

992. **When children were brought to Jesus that He might put His hands on them, His disciples** [Matthew 19:13]
 a   thanked the people
 b   rebuked the people
 c   rebuked the children
 d   said nothing

993. **Jesus said that it is easier for a camel to go through the eye of a needle than for** [Matthew 19:24]
 a   a sinner to exit from hell
 b   any man to observe all Ten Commandments
 c   a rich man to enter into the Kingdom of God
 d   the disciples to judge all men rightly

994. **The number of the disciples, twelve,** [Matthew 19:28]
 a   did not link up with any other number twelve
 b   did link up with another number twelve
 c   linked up with twice times a number six
 d   had no linkage with any other number, twelve or otherwise

995. **"So the last shall be first, and the first last," said Jesus, illustrating this by** [Matthew 20:1–16]
 a   the difficulty encountered by rich men in entering heaven
 b   the thrones to be given to the disciples in the new world

    c children: "of such is the kingdom of heaven"
    d the householder who paid those who worked eleven hours just what he paid those who worked one hour

996. **When the two blind men cried out to Jesus for mercy, the crowd**   [Matthew 20:29–31]
    a rebuked them
    b pleaded for them
    c did not hear them
    d gave them coins

997. **Jesus entered Jerusalem, says Matthew 21, riding on**
                                   [Matthew 21:1–7]
    a a horse
    b an ass
    c a colt
    d an ass and a colt

998. **Jesus entered the temple of God and overthrew the**   [Matthew 21:12]
    a seats of those who sold doves
    b tables of the moneychangers
    c tables of the moneychangers and the seats of those who sold doves
    d seats of the moneychangers

999. **"Out of the mouth of babes and sucklings," said Jesus, referring to what the children had said in the form of**   [Matthew 21:15–16]
    a praise
    b incisive description
    c criticism
    d denunciation

1000. **When Jesus left the temple He went out of Jerusalem to**   [Matthew 21:17]
    a Bethany
    b Bethphage
    c Capernaum
    d Nazareth

1001. **"And all things whatsoever ye shall ask in prayer, believing, ye shall receive," Jesus said to His disciples, after they had marveled at how He had caused a**   [Matthew 21:19–22]
    a mountain to be removed and cast into the sea
    b fig tree to wither
    c stream to dry up
    d sow to eat pearls

1002. **The parable of the two sons whose words did not match their deeds illustrated Jesus' prediction that the chief priest and elders would go into the Kingdom of God**   [Matthew 21:23, 28–32]

  a before the harlots and publicans
  b along with the harlots and publicans
  c after the harlots and publicans
  d after the harlots but before the publicans

1003. **When asked what the absentee landlord should have done to his vineyard tenants (husbandmen) after they had killed his son who had come to collect the rent, the scribes and the Pharisees replied that he should have** [Matthew 21:33–41, 45]

  a simply dispossessed them
  b let the law take its course
  c put them to death
  d forgiven them

1004. **Jesus' words, "For many are called, but few are chosen," were uttered after reciting the parable of the** [Matthew 22:1–14]

  a vineyard tenants
  b vineyard laborers
  c marriage feast
  d two sons

1005. **"Render therefore unto Caesar the things which are Caesar's," said Jesus (when the Pharisees sought to trap Him), referring to** [Matthew 22:15–21]

  a baring one's head before the imperial procession
  b paying the imperial tribute
  c the disposition of Caesar's children
  d Galilee

1006. **The question put by the Sadducees, to which of the seven brothers whom she married successively will the woman be married in heaven? Jesus answered: in the resurrection** [Matthew 22:23–33]

  a the first brother would be her husband
  b she would have her choice
  c the cycle would be repeated indefinitely
  d they do not marry, but are as the angels of God in heaven

1007. **The two great commandments, on which hang all the law and the prophets, as given by Jesus, in Matthew 22, have as their central theme** [Matthew 22:34–40]

  a love
  b obedience
  c respect
  d courage

1008. **As to the scribes and the Pharisees, said Jesus to the multitude and His disciples, do** [Matthew 23:1–7]

  a what they do, not what they say
  b what they say, not what they do
  c neither what they say nor what they do
  d what they do and do what they say

1009. **"Ye blind guides! which strain at a gnat and swallow a camel," said Jesus, referring to the Pharisees'**
[Matthew 23:16-24]
a   unseemly eating habits
b   doctrinal hairsplitting
c   tithing while neglecting weightier matters
d   penny-pinching at the cost of poor quality

1010. **"Woe unto you, scribes and Pharisees, hypocrites! for ye are like unto whited sepulchres," said Jesus, that is,**
[Matthew 23:27-28]
a   white on the outside, black on the inside
b   outwardly beautiful, inwardly foul
c   a formidable structure enclosing nothing
d   giving off surface light, destroying inward light

1011. **The scribes and Pharisees' building of tombs for the prophets and garnishing of sepulchres of the righteous were regarded by Jesus with** [Matthew 23:29-36]
a   approbation
b   indifference
c   astonishment
d   contempt

1012. **"There shall not be left here one stone upon another," said Jesus, referring to Jerusalem's** [Matthew 24:1-2]
a   wall
b   palace
c   temple
d   gate

1013. **To the disciples' question, "What shall be the sign of thy coming, and of the end of the world?" Jesus' reply at first** [Matthew 24:1-26]
a   hinted at the exact date
b   suggested that only the Father knew the sign
c   warned against false Christs and false prophets
d   was one of reproof for asking

1014. **As one of the signs that the coming will be near, said Jesus, the sun will** [Matthew 24:29]
a   be darkened
b   blaze around its rim
c   explode
d   stop

1015. **The coming, said Jesus, will resemble the flood in the days of Noe (Noah) in that** [Matthew 24:36-44]
a   one man will be informed beforehand
b   it will extend over forty days and nights
c   it will come when it is not expected
d   two of each species will be saved

1016. **The five wise virgins who took oil for their lamps turned out to have an advantage over the five foolish virgins, for the bridegroom** [Matthew 25:1-12]

a   had no lamp
b   had no oil
c   feared the dark
d   was delayed

1017.   "For unto every one that hath shall be given . . . but
from him that hath not shall be taken away even that
which he hath," refers, in the second parable in Matthew 25, to   [Matthew 25:14–30]
a   property
b   friendship
c   understanding
d   health

1018.   At the second coming, when the Son of man will divide
the sheep from the goats, one will naturally hope to
find himself classified as   [Matthew 25:31–46]
a   a sheep
b   a goat
c   neither a sheep nor a goat
d   either a sheep or a goat

1019.   Those on His left hand at the day of judgment the Son
of man will condemn to fire for
[Matthew 25:41, 46]
a   seven years
b   forty years
c   an indefinite period
d   eternity

1020.   When the woman in Bethany had poured very expen-
sive ointment on Jesus' head, and the disciples had
protested, Jesus' phrase, "For ye have the poor always
with you," implied that the woman had acted
[Matthew 26:6–13]
a   disgracefully
b   thoughtlessly
c   hypocritically
d   well

1021.   The disciple Judas Iscariot promised to deliver Jesus
over to the chief priests in return for pieces of silver to
the number of   [Matthew 26:14–16]
a   seven
b   thirty
c   forty
d   one hundred and thirty

1022.   At the Last Supper, Jesus predicted that He would be
betrayed by that one of His disciples who had
[Matthew 26:23]
a   entered the room ahead of Him
b   passed Him the dish
c   dipped his hand in the dish with Him
d   finished the meal ahead of Him

1023.   When Peter protested that he would never be "offended"
        as Jesus had predicted all the apostles would be, Jesus
        replied, "Verily I say unto thee, That this night, before
        the cock crow, thou shalt deny me
                                        [Matthew 26:33–34]

        a   once"
        b   twice"
        c   thrice"
        d   four times"

1024.   "The spirit indeed is willing, but the flesh is weak," said
        Jesus, addressing   [Matthew 26:36–37, 40–41]
        a   James
        b   Judas
        c   Peter
        d   Pilate

1025.   "If it be possible, let this cup pass from me!" said, in
        Gethsemane,   [Matthew 26:36, 39]
        a   Jesus
        b   Judas
        c   Peter
        d   Pilate

1026.   Judas betrayed to the crowd that came from the chief
        priests and elders which one was Jesus by
                                        [Matthew 26:47–49]
        a   pointing to Him
        b   kissing Him
        c   taking Him by the hand
        d   describing Him

1027.   "For all they that take the sword, shall perish with the
        sword," said Jesus to   [Matthew 26:51–52]
        a   the crowd of chief priests and elders
        b   a military guard
        c   one of those who were with Jesus
        d   no one in particular

1028.   The chief priests, and elders, and all the council
        reacted adversely on the grounds of what
                                        [Matthew 26:59–68]
        a   false witnesses asserted Jesus had said
        b   true witnesses asserted Jesus had done
        c   Jesus said to them
        d   Jesus refused to say

1029.   Peter denied knowing Jesus, when questioned by
                                        [Matthew 26:69–75]
        a   the high priests and council
        b   Pilate
        c   Jesus
        d   bystanders

1030. **Pilate the governor obtained possession of Jesus from the chief priests and the elders by**   [Matthew 27:1–2]
    a   stealth
    b   force
    c   their own action
    d   means unspecified

1031. **When Judas saw that Jesus was condemned, he went**
                         [Matthew 27:3–5]
    a   into exile
    b   and hanged himself
    c   to Pilate, to appeal
    d   mad

1032. **The chief priests took Judas' discarded pieces of silver and with this blood money bought the potter's field, wherein to bury**   [Matthew 27:6–7]
    a   those with no relatives
    b   the poor
    c   criminals
    d   strangers

1033. **When Pilate asked Jesus, "Art thou the King of the Jews?" Jesus replied**   [Matthew 27:11]
    a   "Yea"
    b   "No"
    c   "Thou sayest"
    d   not at all

1034. **Accustomed at this feast to release any one prisoner the multitude wanted him to, Pilate suggested to them a choice beween Barabbas and Jesus, partly because**
                         [Matthew 27:15–23]
    a   Barabbas was a relative of his
    b   he thought they would choose Jesus
    c   he was in the power of the high priests
    d   his wife had had a dream that day

1035. **Pilate took water and washed his hands before the crowd, to**   [Matthew 27:24]
    a   ratify their choice of Barabbas
    b   indicate that he was innocent of Jesus' blood
    c   clean them of the blood that had come upon them
    d   follow the usual ritual

1036. **Pilate's soldiers put on Jesus a scarlet robe and a crown of thorns,**   [Matthew 27:27–31]
    a   as the crucifixion ritual demanded
    b   at Pilate's express order
    c   to mock Him
    d   in defiance of Pilate

1037. **Jesus' cross was carried to the place of crucifixion, says Matthew, by**   [Matthew 27:32]
    a   Jesus

b   the soldiers
c   a bystander
d   one of the disciples

1038.   **Golgotha is the place where Jesus was**
                                    [Matthew 27:33–35]

a   crucified
b   scourged
c   covered with the crown of thorns
d   buried

1039.   **After they had crucified Jesus, the soldiers cast lots, to determine**   [Matthew 27:35]
a   who would stand watch over Him
b   how they should divide His garments among themselves
c   what other two would be crucified alongside Jesus
d   who would report to the captain

1040.   **The chief priests, the scribes and the elders mocked Jesus upon the cross, and the two thieves crucified with Him**   [Matthew 27:41–44]
a   cursed the priests, scribes and elders
b   offered Jesus consolation
c   mocked Jesus
d   remained silent

1041.   **"My God, my God, why hast thou forsaken me?" cried**
                                    [Matthew 27:46]

a   Jesus
b   Mary
c   Peter
d   a soldier

1042.   **Thereupon a man ran, took a sponge, put it on a reed, and gave it to Jesus to drink, after having filled it with**
                                    [Matthew 27:48]

a   wine mixed with gall
b   vinegar
c   water
d   new wine

1043.   **When Jesus yielded up His spirit, there came at once a great**   [Matthew 27:51–54]
a   deluge
b   earthquake
c   thunderstorm
d   freeze

1044.   **The body of Jesus was placed in a tomb by**
                                    [Matthew 27:57–60]

a   the soldiers
b   the priests
c   His mother and Mary Magdalene
d   a rich man from Arimathaea

1045. **The chief priests and the Pharisees sealed Jesus' tomb for they thought they could thereby prevent**
[Matthew 27:62–66]
   a   His resurrection
   b   the disciples from removing His body
   c   the mob from seizing His body
   d   the people from ever knowing whether Jesus did escape the tomb

1046. **When Mary Magdalene and "the other Mary" were met by Jesus who had risen from the dead, He asked them to inform**   [Matthew 28:1, 9–10]
   a   Pilate
   b   the priests and elders
   c   the disciples
   d   no one, for the time being

1047. **At the mountain in Galilee, Jesus instructed the eleven disciples to**   [Matthew 28:16–20]
   a   bring to justice the priests who had condemned Him
   b   confine their proselytizing efforts to the Jewish peoples
   c   counter the false news spread by the soldiers at the command of the priests and elders
   d   teach and baptize all nations

St. Mark

1048. **According to Mark, Jesus' renown in Capernaum was initiated largely by His power to**   [Mark 1:21–27]
   a   cure paralytics at a distance
   b   cast out unclean spirits
   c   command thunderstorms
   d   recruit disciples

1049. **When the Pharisees questioned Jesus about His disciples' plucking ears of grain on the Sabbath, Jesus said that**
[Mark 2:23–28]
   a   "The sabbath was made for man, and not man for the sabbath"
   b   "Man was made for the sabbath, not the sabbath for man"
   c   "The sabbath was made for man, not for God"
   d   "The sabbath was made for God, not for man"

1050.   **In Mark, Jesus commanded the sea to be still**
                                            [Mark 4:35–41]
        a   as He walked toward the boat, from the shore
        b   immediately after He got into the boat
        c   while Peter was attempting to walk on the water
        d   without His having left the boat

1051.   **"My name is Legion; for we are many," referred to**
                                            [Mark 5:9–15; Luke 8:30]
        a   the disciples
        b   the unclean spirits and the man who harbored them
        c   the lepers in the leper colony
        d   the crowd to whom Jesus spoke by the sea

1052.   **When John reported to Jesus that the disciples had
        ordered a certain man to cease his casting out of devils
        in Jesus' name, because he was not following the dis-
        ciples, Jesus**   [Mark 9:38–41]
        a   approved
        b   disapproved
        c   inquired further
        d   offered no comment

1053.   **The parable of the man with the vineyard differs in
        Mark from the version in Matthew (see No. 1003) in
        that in Mark's version**   [Mark 12:9; Matthew 21:40–41]
        a   the owner's son is not killed
        b   Jesus says the landlord will thereupon destroy the
            tenants
        c   the tenants kill the owner's son for a different reason
        d   none of the servants is killed

1054.   **To the question, which commandment is the first of
        all, Jesus' answer, "thou shalt love the Lord thy God
        with . . . ," as given in Mark differs slightly from
        that in Matthew, by**   [Mark 12:28–30; Matthew 22:37]
        a   omitting "all thy mind"
        b   omitting "all thy heart"
        c   adding "all thy spirit"
        d   adding "all thy strength"

1055.   **The scribe who was, said Jesus, "not far from the
        kingdom of God," achieved this status because he said
        that to love as Jesus asked was**   [Mark 12:33–34]
        a   more than all whole burnt offerings and sacrifices
        b   what he felt to be natural
        c   something he would enjoy encouraging others to do
        d   superhuman

1056.   **When Jesus, watching the people cast money into the
        treasury, saw many that were rich cast in much and
        a poor widow throw in two mites (a farthing), He re-
        marked that the widow's contribution was**
                                            [Mark 12:41–44]
        a   less than the others'

b   equal to the others'
c   more than the others'
d   in no way comparable to the others'

1057. **As to the troubled times to come, Jesus did not say (in Mark) that**   [Mark 13:12]
a   the brother will betray the brother to death
b   the father will betray the son to death
c   the husband will betray his wife to death
d   children will rise up against their parents, and cause their death

1058. **According to Mark 15, at Golgotha Jesus was given wine mingled with**   [Mark 15:23]
a   myrrh
b   gall
c   vinegar
d   water

St. Luke

1059. **The gospel according to Luke relates that the priest Zacharias did not believe the angel Gabriel's announcement that Elisabeth would bear a son, since she was**
                                                    [Luke 1:13–20]
a   a virgin
b   not yet born
c   old
d   a Gentile

1060. **Because Zacharias did not believe the angel Gabriel, he was struck**   [Luke 1:19–23]
a   deaf
b   blind
c   dumb
d   down

1061. **When Mary entered the house of Zacharias and greeted her cousin Elisabeth, the babe leaped in**
                                                    [Luke 1:36, 39–44]
a   Mary's womb
b   Elisabeth's womb
c   both their wombs
d   in neither's womb

1062. **Elisabeth and Zacharias' child was named**
                                                    [Luke 1:57–63]
a   Zacharias

    b   David
    c   John
    d   Elisabeth

1063.   **Mary and Joseph went from Nazareth to Bethlehem for taxation (enrollment) of Joseph, because**
                                                        [Luke 2:4–6]
    a   it had been the city of David
    b   Micah had foretold Bethlehem as the birthplace of Israel's ruler
    c   the three wise men had come there
    d   everyone had to go to his own birthplace

1064.   **Mary wrapped her baby in swaddling clothes and laid him in a manger, because**   [Luke 2:7]
    a   it had so been prophesied
    b   there was no room for them in the inn
    c   they were too poor to lodge in the inn
    d   the three wise men were coming to the manger

1065.   **The shepherds in the field at night were directed to the place where the infant Jesus lay by**   [Luke 2:8–12]
    a   a star
    b   three wise men
    c   an angel
    d   an inner light

1066.   **"Lord, now lettest thou thy servant depart in peace," said**   [Luke 2:25–29]
    a   the shepherd who was needed by his flock
    b   Mary, after the birth of Jesus
    c   Simeon, who was not to see death before he had seen the Lord's Christ
    d   Anna, the eighty-four-year-old prophetess

1067.   **The home city of Joseph and Mary was**   [Luke 2:39]
    a   Jerusalem
    b   Nazareth
    c   Bethlehem
    d   Capernaum

1068.   **When the boy Jesus stayed in Jerusalem, sitting among the doctors in the temple, both hearing them and asking them questions, he was**   [Luke 2:42–49]
    a   eight years old
    b   ten years old
    c   twelve years old
    d   fourteen years old

1069.   **"The voice of one crying in the wilderness" was that of**   [Luke 3:2–4]
    a   John the Baptist
    b   Jesus
    c   Zacharias
    d   Simeon

1070. **John the Baptist instructed the publicans who came to be baptized to** [Luke 3:12–13]
  a   leave their positions
  b   give the tax revenues to the poor
  c   exact no more than that which was appointed them
  d   exact according to ability to pay

1071. **When Jesus began his public ministry he was about**
  [Luke 3:23]
  a   twelve years of age
  b   twenty-four years of age
  c   thirty years of age
  d   thirty-three years of age

1072. **The phrase, "Physician, heal thyself," was uttered in the synagogue by** [Luke 4:22–23]
  a   one of those present, and addressed to Jesus
  b   Jesus, and addressed to those present
  c   Jesus, and addressed to Jesus, but attributed to those present
  d   one of those present, and addressed to Jesus, but attributed to those present

1073. **In Luke 5, Jesus' statement, "Fear not; from henceforth thou shalt catch men," was occasioned by the fact that the four disciples had just caught**
  [Luke 5:1–10]
  a   no fish
  b   one fish
  c   an ordinary number of fish
  d   an extraordinary number of fish

1074. **"And if ye lend to them of whom ye hope to receive," said Jesus, "what thank have ye?" for** [Luke 6:34]
  a   sinners lend to the righteous
  b   the righteous lend to sinners
  c   the righteous lend to the righteous
  d   sinners lend to sinners

1075. **The women specifically listed as accompanying Jesus in His preaching did not, according to Luke, include**
  [Luke 8:2–3]
  a   Mary Magdalene
  b   Mary, the mother of Jesus
  c   Joanna, the wife of Herod's steward
  d   Susanna

1076. **"And it came to pass, when the time was come that he should be received up, he stedfastly set his face to go to Jerusalem," and upon sending messengers ahead to a village of the Samaritans, Jesus learned that He would there be given** [Luke 9:51–56]
  a   a warm reception
  b   a civil reception

    c   no reception

    d   a reception that depended on what He would pay

1077. **"No man, having put his hand to the plough, and looking back, is fit for the kingdom of God," said Jesus, in reply to the man who would follow Him but desired first to** [Luke 9:61-62]

    a   go and bury his dead father

    b   bid farewell to those at his home

    c   save some money to support himself as a disciple

    d   fast and pray to see if he were truly called

1078. **The man left half-dead by thieves on the road from Jerusalem to Jericho was aided by the good Samaritan only after he had been ignored by** [Luke 10:30-37]

    a   one passerby

    b   two passersby

    c   three passersby

    d   fourteen passersby

1079. **"Martha, Martha, thou art careful and troubled about many things," said Jesus, in** [Luke 10:38-42]

    a   sympathy

    b   friendly curiosity

    c   mild reproof

    d   severe judgment

1080. **The version of the Lord's Prayer given in Luke 11 is, compared with that in Matthew 6,**

                  [Luke 11:2-4; Matthew 6:9-13]

    a   shorter

    b   longer

    c   about the same length

    d   shorter in words but longer in letters

1081. **"Ask, and it shall be given you," said Jesus, after illustrating the relative power of** [Luke 11:5-9]

    a   friendship

    b   insolence

    c   importunity

    d   forgetfulness

1082. **Jesus' parable of the rich man who would build greater barns to store his excess produce showed how fruitless was this plan, since** [Luke 12:13-21]

    a   each greater barn excites a desire for one still greater

    b   many more smaller barns spread the risk

    c   rich men copy each other

    d   he would not live to enjoy his produce

1083. **The parable of the servants, one of whom knew his lord's will, while the other did not, showed that, of every one to whom much is given** [Luke 12:41-48]

    a   to him still more will be given

b   to him no more will be given
c   of him much will be required
d   of him little will be required

1084. To His own question, "Or those eighteen, upon whom
the tower in Siloam fell, and slew them, think ye that
they were sinners above all men that dwelt in Jerusalem?" Jesus answered,   [Luke 13:4–5]
a   no
b   yes
c   perhaps
d   there is no way to tell

1085. When Jesus made straight the woman who had been
bowed together for eighteen years, He was criticized by
the ruler of the synagogue for   [Luke 13:10–17]
a   using magic
b   healing on the Sabbath
c   provoking envy
d   healing in the synagogue

1086. When you are invited to a marriage feast, said Jesus,
go and sit in the lowest room (place) so that you may
[Luke 14:7–11]
a   appear not covetous of the bride
b   leave early without disturbing others
c   allow the lowly to be seated above their expectations
d   avoid the shame of being moved down and have
a chance of being moved up

1087. When you give a dinner or a banquet, said Jesus, in-
vite not your friends, brethren, kinsmen, or rich neigh-
bors, but the poor, the maimed, the lame, and the
blind, so that you will not be   [Luke 14:12–14]
a   recompensed by the former group
b   perplexed, whom to omit for lack of room
c   tempted into setting a luxurious table
d   induced to keep late hours

1088. "For which of you," said Jesus, "intending to build a
tower, sitteth not down first, and counteth the cost,
whether he have sufficient to finish it?" referring to
one's decision whether to   [Luke 14:25–33]
a   give a dinner or a banquet
b   emigrate
c   become a disciple of Jesus
d   start guerrilla warfare against Herod

1089. To the parable of the man who rejoiced more over
finding the one lost sheep than over keeping the other
ninety-nine, Jesus added, in Luke 15, the parable of the
lost   [Luke 15:3–10; Matthew 18:12–14]
a   tax receipt
b   lamp

    c   coin
    d   ox

1090. **The thoughts of the Prodigal Son, at the time he was
starving in the fields where he fed swine, make his
father's later reception seem the more**

                                         [Luke 15:11–24]

    a   appropriate
    b   inappropriate
    c   irrelevant
    d   capricious

1091. **The Prodigal Son's brother was evidently somewhat**

                                         [Luke 15:25–32]

    a   dull
    b   forgetful
    c   self-righteous
    d   detached

1092. **Lazarus was a**   [Luke 16:20]
    a   rich man
    b   doorman
    c   beggar man
    d   thief

1093. **After death Lazarus was**   [Luke 16:22]
    a   sent to Hades
    b   carried into Abraham's bosom
    c   raised from the dead
    d   buried in the lepers' cemetery

1094. **Does the master thank the servant because he did what
was commanded? asked Jesus, implying that the answer
is clearly**   [Luke 17:9–10]
    a   no
    b   yes
    c   sometimes no, sometimes yes
    d   it all depends

1095. **The Samaritan leper was appreciated by Jesus because
he gave**   [Luke 17:11–19]
    a   help without thanks
    b   thanks for help
    c   help and thanks
    d   help for thanks

1096. **The parable of the unjust judge who decided to avenge
the widow of her adversary was evidently meant to be**
                                         [Luke 18:1–8]
    a   encouraging
    b   discouraging
    c   confusing
    d   admonishing

1097. The Pharisee who gave thanks to God that he was not
       like other men was viewed by Jesus with
                                              [Luke 18:10–14]
       a   approbation
       b   disapprobation
       c   pity
       d   relief

1098. The rich publican Zacchaeus climbed up into a syca-
       more tree because he was   [Luke 19:2–4]
       a   pursued
       b   mad
       c   warm
       d   short

1099. The parable of the servants left with their master's
       money to handle shows the danger of excessive
                                              [Luke 19:12–26]
       a   apprehension
       b   speculation
       c   illegality
       d   deviousness

1100. "The stones would immediately cry out," said Jesus, if
       the disciples   [Luke 19:37–40]
       a   acted unjustly
       b   betrayed Him
       c   held their peace
       d   used violence

1101. When Jesus said, "But there shall not an hair of your
       head perish," He was speaking   [Luke 21:10–19]
       a   literally
       b   figuratively
       c   in hyperbola
       d   paradoxically

1102. When strife developed at the Last Supper among the
       twelve disciples as to which of them should be accounted
       the greatest, Jesus said, "he that is greatest among you,
       let him be as the   [Luke 22:24–26]
       a   younger"
       b   older"
       c   weaker"
       d   stronger"

1103. In the account by Luke, compared with those by Mat-
       thew and Mark, Pilate's attitude toward Jesus is ap-
       preciably more
             [Luke 23:1–25; Matthew 27:11–26; Mark 15:1–15]
       a   sympathetic
       b   callous
       c   ambivalent
       d   indifferent

1104. **Jesus became the indirect instrument of making Pilate and Herod** [Luke 23:12]
   a   enemies
   b   friends
   c   acquaintances
   d   rivals

1105. **Jesus uttered the cry, "Father, forgive them; for they know not what they do," when He was**
                                                    [Luke 23:33–34]
   a   before the crowd that shouted to crucify Him
   b   officially condemned by Pilate
   c   crucified
   d   scoffed at by bystanders

1106. **Luke differs from Matthew and Mark with respect to the two malefactors crucified with Jesus by stating that**
                      [Luke 23:39–43; Matthew 27:44; Mark 15:32]
   a   one of them railed on Jesus, while the other remained silent
   b   both of them praised Jesus
   c   one of them railed on Jesus and was rebuked by the other
   d   one of them praised Jesus and was rebuked by the other

1107. **According to Luke, that which Mary Magdalene, Joanna, and Mary the mother of James, and the other women that were with them, told the apostles, and which they did not believe, was that they had**
                                                    [Luke 24:1–11]
   a   seen the resurrected Jesus
   b   found the sepulchre empty
   c   listened to an angel clothed in a long white garment
   d   been helped back along the road by centurions

1108. **The resurrected Christ vanished before the eyes of the men with whom He walked on the road to Emmaus immediately after** [Luke 24:13–16, 30–31]
   a   they expressed doubt that what the prophets had spoken would occur
   b   they invited Him to stay with them
   c   they reported what the women had found at the tomb
   d   He blessed bread, broke it, and gave it to them

1109. **When the resurrected Jesus stood among His apostles, the methods He used to persuade them that He was not a spirit did not include** [Luke 24:36–43]
   a   urging them to regard His hands and feet
   b   healing one of the bystanders who had leprosy
   c   inviting them to handle Him, since a spirit has not flesh and bones
   d   asking them for something to eat, and eating it

1110. **Jesus vanished from the apostles as they reached the town of**   [Luke 24:50–51]
   a Bethany
   b Bethlehem
   c Capernaum
   d Nazareth

St. John

1111. **The gospel according to John begins with**
                                              [John 1:1–15]

   a a genealogy of Jesus
   b a quotation from Isaiah
   c an explanation of why he is writing this narrative
   d a paean to the Word

1112. **John's account of how the first two disciples of Jesus were chosen does not differ from that of Matthew's with respect to the**   [John 1:35–42; Matthew 4:18–20]
   a place
   b manner of meeting Jesus
   c activity they were engaged in at the time
   d name of one of these two disciples being Andrew

1113. **At the wedding in Cana of Galilee, Jesus caused the six waterpots of stone, each holding two or three firkins, to contain**   [John 2:1–9]
   a water instead of wine
   b nothing instead of water
   c wine instead of nothing
   d wine instead of water

1114. **Jesus drove the traders and the moneychangers from the temple with a**   [John 2:14–15]
   a knife
   b sword
   c bludgeon
   d scourge

1115. **When Jesus said that He would raise up the temple in three days if it were destroyed, He was referring to**
                                              [John 2:18–22]

   a the temple, literally
   b His body
   c the activities within the temple
   d a primitive form of the temple

1116. **"The wind bloweth where it listeth," said Jesus to**
[John 3:4–8]
   - a   Philip
   - b   His mother, Mary
   - c   Nicodemus
   - d   Peter

1117. **The gospel of St. John teaches that God sent His only Son into the world because of God's** [John 3:15]
   - a   anger with the world
   - b   puzzlement with the world
   - c   love of the world
   - d   love of His Son

1118. **John the Baptist compared himself to a**
[John 3:28–30]
   - a   father of the bride
   - b   bridegroom
   - c   friend of the bridegroom
   - d   officiating minister

1119. **The Samaritan woman at the well, whom Jesus asked for a drink, gave** [John 4:7–29]
   - a   Him water from the well
   - b   Him directions for assistance
   - c   others her belief in His divinity
   - d   Him warning of danger

1120. **"One soweth, and another reapeth," said Jesus, specifying that His disciples were** [John 4:36–38]
   - a   sowers
   - b   reapers
   - c   both sowers and reapers
   - d   neither sowers nor reapers

1121. **Jesus departed again into a mountain, after the miracle of the loaves and the fishes, because He saw (according to John) that the people were about to come and take Him by force, to** [John 6:15]
   - a   crucify Him
   - b   turn Him over to Pilate
   - c   make Him feed all their relatives
   - d   make Him a king

1122. **When Jesus had walked on the water during the night to join His disciples in the ship going across the sea, the people on the shore the next day** [John 6:17–24]
   - a   did not notice that He had left
   - b   assumed that He had started off in the ship
   - c   sensed something puzzling, and sought Him in Capernaum
   - d   took it for granted that He could have walked on the water

1123. **Jesus' brothers ("brethren"—see No. 971)** [John 7:5]
    a believed in Him
    b did not believe in Him
    c differed among themselves as to belief in Him
    d did not raise the question for themselves

1124. **Jesus said to His brethren, while He was still in Galilee, that the world hated Him because He** [John 7:7]
    a offered salvation only to those who believed in Him
    b performed miracles
    c welcomed repentant sinners
    d testified that its works were evil

1125. **After Jesus' proclamation on the last day of the feast in Jerusalem, some were still doubtful that He was the Christ, because He had** [John 7:41, 52]
    a performed few miracles
    b come from Galilee
    c no outward sign from heaven
    d cured a man on the Sabbath

1126. **Nicodemus implied that Jesus should be judged**
    [John 7:50–51]
    a without a hearing
    b only after a hearing
    c after hearing third parties
    d not at all

1127. **"He that is without sin among you, let him first cast a stone" at the woman taken in adultery, said Jesus, evidently expecting** [John 8:1–9]
    a that the sinful would thereby reveal themselves
    b that they would turn to stone Him
    c to foil the scribes and Pharisees who hoped to have some grounds for accusing Him
    d the woman to assert that she had committed no sin

1128. **"And the truth shall make you free," said Jesus, meaning, free from** [John 8:31–36]
    a the rule of Herod
    b misconceptions of Jesus' role
    c servitude to sin
    d the dictates of the Old Testament

1129. **"There is no truth in him," said Jesus, referring to**
    [John 8:44]
    a the devil
    b the high priest
    c Pilate
    d Judas Iscariot

1130. **When His disciples asked Him who had sinned, that the man they saw had been blind from birth, Jesus said**
    [John 9:1–3]
    a the man himself

  b his parents
  c all the world
  d that it was not a question of sinning, at all

1131. **Upon being questioned, the parents of the man Jesus cured of his blindness said they did not know who had opened his eyes, because they** [John 9:18–23]
  a in fact did not know
  b had promised Jesus not to tell
  c were superstitious
  d feared the displeasure of their questioners

1132. **The man himself, upon being requestioned,**
                                                        [John 9:24–34]
  a pointed out that if Jesus were not of God, He could not have opened his eyes
  b agreed that it might have been a coincidence
  c said that he suspected Jesus obtained His powers from the devil
  d refused to discuss the matter further

1133. **A good shepherd, said Jesus, will be so** [John 10:7–18]
  a adored by his sheep that they will lay down their lives for him
  b concerned for his sheep that he will lay down his life for them
  c united with his sheep that he and they will die to-together
  d skillful that neither he nor his sheep will die

1134. **Those who stoned Jesus told Him they did so because, being** [John 10:31–33]
  a a part of God, He yet appeared in the form of a man
  b a descendant of David, He yet refused to accept the Old Testament rules
  c a man, He made Himself God
  d a layman, He spoke in the temple

1135. **Jesus started for Judaea when He heard Lazarus was ill,**
                                                        [John 11:5–15]
  a immediately
  b after one day
  c after two days
  d after three days

1136. **Bethany was distant from Jerusalem about** [John 11:18]
  a two miles
  b five miles
  c nine miles
  d fourteen miles

1137. **"I am the resurrection, and the life," said Jesus to**
                                                        [John 11:24–25]
  a Lazarus

    b   Martha
    c   Mary
    d   no one in particular

1138. "Jesus wept," when He   [John 11:33–35]
    a   heard of Lazarus' illness
    b   met Martha, Lazarus' sister, as He came to Bethany
    c   saw Mary and the Jews who came with her, weeping
    d   came to the cave

1139. When Jesus said, "Take ye away the stone" from the cave, Martha objected that, since Lazarus had been dead four days,   [John 11:39]
    a   his features would be unsightly
    b   there would be an odor
    c   the grave cloths would have rotted
    d   it might prove too late

1140. As John relates it, the chief priests and the Pharisees were primarily worried that, if they allowed Jesus to perform more miracles, everyone would believe in Him, and then   [John 11:48]
    a   no one would believe in them
    b   they would have to pretend to believe in Him
    c   missionaries of the new faith would emigrate
    d   the Romans would come and take away their place and nation

1141. Judas Iscariot takes on an additional attribute in the gospel according to John: he is described as
                             [John 12:4–6]
    a   an extortioner
    b   a thief
    c   a burglar
    d   a confidence man

1142. Because he had been raised from the dead, Lazarus was
                          [John 12:9–11]
    a   assured of a long life
    b   in imminent danger of being put to death
    c   liable to contract diseases
    d   uncertain of his friends

1143. When the many people who had come for the passover feast went out to meet Jesus as He rode toward Jerusalem on an ass's colt, the Pharisees were
                          [John 12:12–19]
    a   encouraged
    b   discouraged
    c   ecstatic
    d   noncommittal

1144. When at the Last Supper Jesus girded Himself with a towel, poured water into a basin and began to wash the disciples' feet and to wipe them with that towel, the disciple that protested against having his feet washed by Jesus was   [John 13:1–8]

a Peter
b Matthew
c Philip
d Judas

1145. **Jesus explained to His disciples that He had washed their feet in order to**   [John 13:12–17]
a prepare Himself for His coming ordeal
b show to the crowd He had no desire to rule
c give the disciples an example of how they should treat one another
d prove that He did not consider Himself their Master

1146. **Jesus' statement that one of the disciples would betray Him was made**   [John 13:4, 18–19, 21–27]
a long before the Last Supper
b just before the Last Supper
c as the Last Supper began
d after rising from the Last Supper

1147. **When, having received from Jesus the dipped sop, Judas disappeared into the night, some of the disciples thought he had gone to**   [John 13:29]
a betray Jesus for twelve pieces of silver
b buy Jesus' freedom
c hang himself
d buy what they needed for the feast, or give to the poor

1148. **"A new commandment I give unto you," said Jesus, "That ye**   [John 13:34]
a spread the gospel"
b love one another"
c confess your sins"
d chastise the unbelievers"

1149. **"In my Father's house are many mansions," said Jesus, implying that**   [John 14:1–4]
a peoples of all backgrounds could aspire to heaven
b once He had gone it would be impossible to trace Him
c He would prepare a place for them
d God was the architect of many worlds

1150. **Upon this remark (see No. 1149) by Jesus, the disciple Thomas**   [John 14:5–7]
a evinced admiration
b expressed doubt
c asked a question
d gave way to anger

1151. **The Disciple Philip said it would suffice them if Jesus would**   [John 14:8]
   a prevent the betrayal
   b bring Pilate to believe
   c show them the Father
   d stay with them three days more

1152. **"Greater love hath no man than this," Jesus said to His disciples, "that a man**   [John 15:13]
   a show his friend the true glory of God"
   b leave family and friends for the faith"
   c return good to his friends for their evil"
   d lay down his life for his friends"

1153. **According to John, when Judas brought the soldiers and officers to seize Jesus, He was identified by**
                                                          [John 18:4–8]
   a a kiss from Judas
   b the description Judas had given them
   c His own words: "I am he"
   d the descent of a dove from heaven

1154. **Malchus was the name of**   [John 18:10]
   a the high priest's servant whose right ear was cut off
   b the captain of the centurions
   c the officer to whom Judas had betrayed Jesus
   d a town near the garden where Jesus was seized

1155. **When the high priest questioned Jesus about His disciples and His doctrine, Jesus**   [John 18:19–21]
   a told him about them, at length
   b referred the priest to those who had heard Him teach
   c informed the priest that it was none of his concern
   d refused to reply at all

1156. **When Pilate told the Jews to take Jesus themselves and judge Him by their own law, they replied that**
                                                          [John 18:28–32]
   a Roman law had precedence in secular matters
   b they could not guarantee Him a fair trial
   c they disagreed about how their law applied to this case
   d it was not lawful for them to put any man to death

1157. **"What is truth?" asked**   [John 18:38]
   a Jesus
   b Pilate
   c Caiaphas
   d Peter

1158. **Pilate said to the Jews, regarding Jesus,**
                                            [John 18:38; 19:4, 6]
   a "I find him guilty of blasphemy"
   b "I find him guilty of fostering public disorder"

c "I find no evidence one way or another"
d "I find no fault in him"

1159. **When Pilate sought to release Jesus, he was met with the argument that**   [John 19:12]
a it would avail nothing: the mob would tear Him in pieces
b it would create a precedent against arresting the apostles
c Pilate would be proven not a friend of Caesar's
d the Pharisees and high priests would emigrate

1160. **According to John, the cross on which Jesus was crucified was borne to Golgotha by**   [John 19:17]
a Jesus Himself
b Simon of Cyrene
c Peter
d centurions

1161. **In Hebrew, Latin, and Greek, Pilate wrote a title and put it on the cross:**   [John 19:19–21]
a "This man said, I am King of the Jews"
b "Jesus of Nazareth the King of the Jews"
c "Jesus of Nazareth, not King of the Jews"
d "King of the Jews"

1162. **"What I have written I have written," said** [John 19:22]
a Pilate
b Jesus
c the high priest
d Peter

1163. **The two angels in white in the empty sepulchre of Jesus were seen by**   [John 20:1–13]
a Peter
b the disciple who had outrun Peter
c Mary Magdalene, before she went to tell Peter that the sepulchre was empty
d Mary Magdalene, after she had told Peter

1164. **Jesus, having left the sepulchre, was first seen by**
                                                    [John 20:14–18]
a Peter
b Mary Magdalene
c His mother, Mary
d the disciple who had outrun Peter

1165. **Upon being told that Jesus had appeared among the other disciples while he was absent, Thomas**
                                                    [John 20:24–25]
a evinced admiration
b expressed doubt
c asked a question
d gave way to anger

1166. Because Jesus, in His third appearance after rising from the dead, asked Simon Peter three times whether he loved Him, Peter was   [John 21:17]
a   overjoyed
b   puzzled
c   grieved
d   angry

The Acts of the Apostles

1167. The Acts of the Apostles, to judge from the opening sentence, was written by   [The Acts 1:1; Luke 1:3]
a   Matthew
b   Mark
c   Luke
d   John

1168. According to The Acts, Jesus appeared to the apostles, after His resurrection, for   [The Acts 1:3]
a   three days
b   twenty days
c   thirty-five days
d   forty days

1169. As the disciples were looking on, Jesus was taken up out of their sight by a   [The Acts 1:9]
a   lightning flash
b   cloud
c   rain storm
d   darkening of the heavens

1170. Peter and John were arrested because the priests, the captain of the temple, and the Sadducees were grieved by their   [The Acts 4:1–3]
a   healing without a license
b   preaching in Solomon's portico
c   preaching through Jesus the resurrection from the dead
d   speaking in foreign tongues

1171. Peter and John were   [The Acts 4:13]
a   both learned

b   both unlearned
c   learned (Peter) and unlearned (John)
d   unlearned (Peter) and learned (John)

1172. **The rulers, elders, scribes, the high priest, and his kindred, after interrogating Peter and John,**
[The Acts 4:13–17]
a   concluded no miracle had been performed
b   were uncertain whether a miracle had been performed
c   agreed that Peter and John had performed a miracle, but feared no repetition
d   agreed that Peter and John had performed a miracle and realized they could repeat

1173. **No punishment was meted out to Peter and John, because those noted in No. 1172** [The Acts 4:17–22]
a   concluded no miracle had been performed
b   contemplated performing the same miracle themselves
c   feared the popular reaction to punishment of the disciples
d   could not agree

1174. **Ananias and his wife Sapphira** [The Acts 5:1–11]
a   both lied and both died
b   both lied, but neither died
c   lied, one of them, and died
d   lied, one of them, whereupon the other died

1175. **When the high priest and the Sadducees had finally imprisoned the apostles, they were released by**
[The Acts 5:17–23]
a   the multitude, who stormed the gates
b   their own faith, which opened the doors
c   an angel of the Lord, who opened the doors
d   the high priest himself, who had developed misgivings

1176. **The Pharisee Gamaliel persuaded his fellow councilmen not to kill the disciples, on the argument that**
[The Acts 5:33–40]
a   new recruits would be attracted by their martyrdom
b   Jesus was indeed the Christ
c   the councilmen would be killed by the enraged multitude
d   if the disciples' work were of men, it would fail; if of God, it could not be overthrown

1177. **The body of the disciples, summoned by the twelve, chose seven (including Stephen) to** [The Acts 6:1–6]
a   argue on behalf of all the disciples, at the council
b   perform the duties called for by the daily ministration

    c set up a network that would aid escapees
    d travel to Thebes

1178. **"Ye stiffnecked, and uncircumcised in**   [The Acts 7:51]
    a eyes and tongue"
    b eyes and ears"
    c heart and ears"
    d heart and eyes"

1179. **While Stephen was being stoned to death, he cried to
the Lord with a loud voice for**   [The Acts 7:59–60]
    a help
    b death
    c vengeance
    d forgiveness

1180. **The aftermath of Stephen's death was a** [The Acts 8:1]
    a lull in the persecution
    b closer grouping of the believers
    c scattering of the believers
    d wave of suicides among the believers

1181. **Candace was**   [The Acts 8:27]
    a queen of the Ethiopians
    b a daughter of Simon
    c high priestess of Egypt
    d a town in Galilee

1182. **Compared with the conversion of the unnamed eunuch
by Philip, that of Saul was**   [The Acts 9:1–18; 8:26–39]
    a peaceful
    b spectacular
    c incomplete
    d complete

1183. **"The street which is called Straight" was that to which
the Lord directed**   [The Acts 9:11]
    a Ananias
    b Philip
    c Saul
    d the eunuch

1184. **The power to raise someone from the dead was**
                                    [The Acts 9:36–43]
    a demonstrated by Peter
    b shown to be not possessed by Peter
    c never tested, for Peter
    d possessed, but not demonstrated, by Peter

1185. **Cornelius of Caesarea, who received instructions from
an angel of God to send to Joppa for Peter, was a**
                                    [The Acts 10:1–8]
    a high priest
    b beggar
    c disciple
    d centurion

1186. **"God is no respecter of persons," said Peter, in connection with a distinction between** [The Acts 10:28–34]
   a   Romans and Palestinians
   b   kings and commoners
   c   Gentiles and Jews
   d   the rich and the poor

1187. **When, during the discussion with Peter at Cornelius' house, the Holy Ghost fell on all those present, the Hebrews there were** [The Acts 10:44–45, 24–27]
   a   unsurprised
   b   astonished
   c   dismayed
   d   not aware of what had happened

1188. **"They that were of the circumcision" in Jerusalem, upon hearing Peter's account of what had happened,**
                                                  [The Acts 11:2–18]
   a   remained completely unconvinced
   b   suggested another trial
   c   split in their opinion
   d   agreed with his interpretation

1189. **Barnabas went to Tarsus** [The Acts 11:25]
   a   at Saul's request
   b   to seek Saul
   c   with Saul
   d   to avoid Saul

1190. **The disciples were for the first time called Christians**
                                                  [The Acts 11:26]
   a   in Antioch
   b   in Tarsus
   c   at Cornelius' house in Caesarea
   d   in Jerusalem

1191. **Herod killed** [The Acts 12:1–2]
   a   Agabus
   b   Barnabas
   c   James
   d   Saul

1192. **Upon Peter's escape from prison, Herod ordered the keepers to** [The Acts 12:18–19]
   a   find him at all costs
   b   remain in prison until he was found
   c   search for the angel of the Lord
   d   be put to death

1193. **The shout of the people praising Herod's oration, "It is the voice of a god, and not of a man," proved to be for him** [The Acts 12:21–23]
   a   a stimulus to more persecution
   b   an inducement to less persecution
   c   a challenge to improve his syntax
   d   unfortunate

1194. **Bar-jesus was**   [The Acts 13:6]
    a a Jewish false prophet
    b another name for Saul
    c another name for Paul
    d a proconsul

1195. **Paul was**   [The Acts 13:9]
    a one of the twelve disciples
    b a convert at Paphos
    c another name for Saul
    d another name for Barnabas

1196. **In his sermon at Antioch of Pisidia, Paul declared that everyone that believes is, by Jesus, justified from all things**   [The Acts 13:38–39, 13–16]
    a except those from which they could not be justified by the law of Moses
    b from which they could be justified by the law of Moses
    c from which they could not be justified by the law of Moses
    d in the law of Moses

1197. **Paul could tell that the man at Lystra who had been crippled from birth had faith enough to be made well, by**   [The Acts 14:8–10]
    a intently following him
    b stedfastly beholding him
    c cautiously approaching him
    d asking an angel

1198. **After some discussion among the apostles and the elders, it was decided that converted Gentiles should not be obliged to**   [The Acts 15:1–29]
    a abstain from meats offered to idols
    b abstain from blood and from things strangled
    c abstain from fornication
    d be circumcised

1199. **Paul and Barnabas separated over a difference of opinion concerning**   [The Acts 15:36–39]
    a circumcision
    b Antioch
    c John (surname, Mark)
    d Silas

1200. **Timotheus was**   [The Acts 16:1–4]
    a the ruler of Lystra
    b a disciple who accompanied Barnabas
    c a disciple who accompanied Paul
    d the husband of Lydia

1201. **Lydia, from Thyatira, was a seller of purple, who**
                                         [The Acts 16:13–15]
    a worshiped God

b   worshiped God and was baptized
c   worshiped God, was baptized, and urged the
    apostles to stay in her house
d   did not worship God

1202. The masters of the damsel possessed with a spirit of
      divination had Paul and Silas thrown in prison, after
      Paul had caused her to cease crying that the apostles
      were   [The Acts 16:16–24]
      a   servants of the most high God
      b   servants of the Baals
      c   in the pay of the Romans
      d   charlatans

1203. When Paul and Silas escaped from prison, their jailer,
      compared with the sentries at Peter's prison, fared
                                              [The Acts 16:25–34]
      a   worse
      b   better
      c   just the same
      d   we are not told how

1204. The magistrates who had imprisoned Paul and Silas be-
      sought them and brought them out, when they learned
      that they were   [The Acts 16:38–39]
      a   truly apostles
      b   not common men
      c   able to sway the multitude
      d   Roman citizens

1205. Paul and Silas were attacked in Thessalonica for acting
      contrary to the decrees of Caesar by saying that
                                              [The Acts 17:4–7]
      a   the son of God was greater than any king
      b   there was another king, Jesus
      c   Caesar was not a true king
      d   Caesar's kingship had passed to Jesus

1206. In Athens, Paul explained that God caused Jesus to be
      raised from the dead to give all men assurance that the
                                              [The Acts 17:30–31]
      a   world would be judged in righteousness by a man
          He had ordained
      b   powers of God were limitless
      c   apostles were a group specially endowed
      d   penalties of this world would be set aside by God

1207. Paul was by trade a   [The Acts 18:1–3]
      a   fisherman
      b   mason
      c   tentmaker
      d   publican

1208. Priscilla was   [The Acts 18:2–3]
      a   a concubine of Claudius

    b   a high priestess at Rome
    c   the wife of a tentmaker
    d   an Epicurean

1209. "Your blood be upon your own heads," said Paul, "from henceforth I will go unto the   [The Acts 18:6]
    a   Gentiles"
    b   Jews"
    c   Greeks"
    d   Corinthians"

1210. At Ephesus John found disciples who had not even heard that there was a Holy Ghost, for they had
    [The Acts 19:1–6]
    a   not been baptized
    b   been baptized only by John the Baptist
    c   been baptized by other than the original twelve disciples
    d   been baptized more than once

1211. The seven sons of Sceva   [The Acts 19:13–16]
    a   succeeded
    b   suffered
    c   stagnated
    d   sentimentalized

1212. The riot at Ephesus was caused by fear that Paul's preaching would create unemployment among
    [The Acts 19:23–29]
    a   policemen
    b   acolytes
    c   silversmiths
    d   mariners

1213. The young man who fell asleep while Paul was speaking at Troas was by Paul   [The Acts 20:6–12]
    a   rebuked
    b   forgiven
    c   ignored
    d   restored to life

1214. "It is more blessed to give than to receive," said
    [The Acts 20:18, 35]
    a   Paul
    b   Jesus, said Paul
    c   Paul, said Silas
    d   Silas

1215. The chief captain of the band and his soldiers, and centurions, by arresting Paul,   [The Acts 21:27–36]
    a   saved him from rioters in Jerusalem
    b   interrupted his progress in converting Gentiles
    c   gave the Romans a source of revenue, through ransom
    d   simply satisfied their own curiosity

1216. **The chief captain in Jerusalem who had ordered that Paul be examined by scourging changed his mind when he learned that Paul was** [The Acts 22:25–29]
    a   truly an apostle
    b   not a common man
    c   able to sway the multitude
    d   a Roman citizen

1217. **Paul was** [The Acts 23:6]
    a   a Pharisee
    b   a Sadducee
    c   neither a Pharisee nor a Sadducee
    d   both a Pharisee and a Sadducee

1218. **Those who bound themselves under a curse neither to eat nor drink until they had killed Paul were frustrated by Paul's** [The Acts 23:12–25]
    a   sister
    b   nephew
    c   uncle
    d   aunt

1219. **The chief captain, in his letter to the Roman governor on Paul's case, in effect requested** [The Acts 23:26–30]
    a   that Paul be exiled
    b   that his would-be assassins be imprisoned
    c   a change of venue
    d   more authority

1220. **In the hearing before Governor Felix, the spokesman for the high priest and the elders, Tertullus, did not call Paul a** [The Acts 24: 2–8]
    a   pestilent fellow
    b   gentilophile
    c   mover of sedition
    d   ringleader

1221. **Felix's conduct toward Paul** [The Acts 24:22–26]
    a   was tinged with pecuniary motives
    b   reflected an agreement with Paul's doctrine
    c   was designed solely to placate Paul's accusers
    d   was harsh in the extreme

1222. **Felix's wife Drusilla was a** [The Acts 24:24]
    a   Gentile
    b   Jewess
    c   Egyptian
    d   Ethiopian

1223. **Felix's successor, Porcius Festus, showed toward Paul's accusers** [The Acts 24:27; 25:9, 12]
    a   less sympathy than Felix
    b   more sympathy than Felix
    c   just about the same degree of sympathy as Felix
    d   no sympathy at all

1224. **Festus brought Paul before King Agrippa**
[The Acts 25:13–27]
   a   as the final judge in Paul's case
   b   as the arbitrator urged by the accusers
   c   to ascertain what could be written to the emperor
   d   because Bernice requested it

1225. **In his defense before King Agrippa, Paul, with respect to his persecution of the saints prior to his famous journey to Damascus,**   [The Acts 26:9–11]
   a   said nothing about it
   b   referred to it incidentally
   c   pleaded irresponsibility
   d   forcefully detailed it, without excusing himself

1226. **Agrippa's reaction to Paul's defense was that Paul's appeal to Caesar was**   [The Acts 26:32]
   a   a shrewd move
   b   the only thing that now kept him from being freed
   c   legally unacceptable
   d   of dubious worth, given the then Caesar

1227. **When the storm along the Cretean coast struck the ship on which Paul was being taken to Italy, the officers first cast overboard**   [The Acts 27:14, 18–19]
   a   Paul
   b   all the prisoners
   c   the cargo
   d   the ship's tackling

1228 **The angel of God that appeared to Paul gave his assurance of safety for**   [The Acts 27:23–24]
   a   himself alone
   b   himself and the centurion Julius, in charge of him
   c   all those on the ship
   d   all on the ship and the ship itself

1229. **The Maltese decided that Paul was a god when he survived despite being**   [The Acts 28:3–6]
   a   trampled by a bull
   b   stoned by the people
   c   struck by lightning
   d   bitten by a viper

1230. **During his stay at Malta, Paul healed**
[The Acts 28:7–10]
   a   no one
   b   only the father of the chief man of the island
   c   all who believed
   d   all who came to him

1231. **Talking to the brethren in Rome, Paul induced belief in**
[The Acts 28:23–25]
   a   none of them
   b   all of them

c   some, while others disbelieved
d   just one

1232.   **During the two years that he lived in Rome at his own
        expense, Paul**   [The Acts 28:30–31]
        a   preached quite openly and unhindered
        b   preached openly, but was hindered appreciably
        c   preached only in secret
        d   did not preach at all

Romans

1233.   **Paul's epistle to the Romans was addressed to**
                                         [Romans 1:7]
        a   residents of Rome
        b   Roman citizens
        c   Roman slaves
        d   Christians at Rome

1234.   **Paul's letter was evidently written**   [Romans 1:10–13]
        a   before he came to Rome
        b   while in Rome
        c   upon leaving Rome
        d   after his return from Rome

1235.   **Paul charged that among those who worshiped images
        resembling mortal man or birds or beasts or creeping
        things there were men who "burned in their lust" for**
                                         [Romans 1:22–23, 27]
        a   gold
        b   harlots
        c   each other
        d   themselves

1236.   **They "are a law unto themselves," said Paul, referring
        to a certain type of Gentile with**   [Romans 2:14–16]
        a   approbation
        b   disapprobation
        c   indifference
        d   puzzlement

1237.   **Can we Jews say that we are better than others? asks
        Paul, and answers,**   [Romans 3:9]
        a   yes
        b   perhaps
        c   perhaps not
        d   not at all

1238. **"Therefore we conclude," said Paul, "that a man is justified**   [Romans 3:28]
    a by faith together with the deeds of the law"
    b by faith without the deeds of the law"
    c by the deeds of the law apart from faith"
    d neither by faith nor by the deeds of the law"

1239. **Abraham's faith in God, said Paul, was reckoned to him as righteousness**   [Romans 4:9–11]
    a before he was circumcised
    b only after he was circumcised
    c at the moment of circumcision
    d when he circumcised others

1240. **Abraham's great virtue, when he considered his own body and Sarah's womb, was to react to God's promise of descendants with**   [Romans 4:16–22]
    a incredulity
    b astonishment
    c faith
    d caution

1241. **Christ, Paul noted, died for the**   [Romans 5:6]
    a righteous
    b good
    c ungodly
    d circumcised

1242. **"For the wages of sin," said Paul, "is**   [Romans 6:23]
    a damnation"
    b darkness"
    c death"
    d destruction"

1243. **"Now if I do that I would not," said Paul, "it is no more I that do it, but**   [Romans 7:20]
    a the devil without"
    b sin that dwelleth in me"
    c the one that tempteth me"
    d my other self"

1244. **Since God "hath . . . mercy on whom he will have mercy, and whom he will he hardeneth," you will ask me, said Paul, " 'Why doth he yet find fault? For who hath resisted his will?' " but the answer to this, continued Paul, is simply that**   [Romans 9:14–21]
    a what is formed can scarcely say to Him who formed it, why have you made me thus?
    b if one refuses to make an effort, he thereby denies God's will
    c God acts in terms of probabilities, under the law of large numbers
    d there need be no answer

1245. **Faith, said Paul, can come** [Romans 10:17]
    a instinctively
    b by divine inspiration
    c by accident
    d from what is heard

1246. **Paul described himself as a member of the tribe of**
[Romans 11:1]
    a Asher
    b Benjamin
    c Judah
    d Reuben

1247. **In the parallel he drew with the olive tree, Paul evidently intended the Gentiles to be the**
[Romans 11:17–24]
    a root
    b natural branches
    c graffed shoot
    d olive

1248. **"Thou shalt heap coals of fire on his head," said Paul, urging his brethren to be** [Romans 12:20]
    a generous to a friend
    b generous to an enemy
    c stern with a friend
    d stern with an enemy

1249. **Vis-à-vis the authorities, Paul counselled**
[Romans 13:1–5]
    a obedience
    b resistance
    c skepticism
    d indifference

1250. **Paul urged his brethren** [Romans 14:13]
    a to pass judgment on one another
    b not to pass judgment on one another
    c to suspend judgment on one another
    d to accept judgment from one another

1251. **After Rome, Paul planned to go to**
[Romans 15:24, 28]
    a Achaia
    b Macedonia
    c Sicily
    d Spain

1252. **The one who wrote this epistle names himself as**
[Romans 16:22]
    a Erastus, the city treasurer
    b Gaius
    c Tertius
    d Paul

1 Corinthians

1253. **Christ sent me, said Paul,**   [1 Corinthians 1:17]
  - a   to baptize and preach the gospel
  - b   not to baptize but to preach the gospel
  - c   to baptize and not to preach the gospel
  - d   not to baptize and not to preach the gospel

1254. **What you build, on the foundation I laid (said Paul), will be tested, on the day, by**   [1 Corinthians 3:10–15]
  - a   fire
  - b   water
  - c   locusts
  - d   ice

1255. **Paul declared that he did not judge himself, because**
      [1 Corinthians 4:3–4]
  - a   he was not aware of anything against him
  - b   he was an evangelist, not to be judged
  - c   brethren judge each other, not themselves
  - d   it is the Lord who judges

1256. **Don't be puffed up, said Paul, for one against another;**
      [1 Corinthians 4:6–7]
  - a   others are better than you
  - b   you don't enjoy boasters
  - c   boasting impairs caution
  - d   what you have, you were given

1257. **"We are made as the filth of the world, and are the offscouring of all things unto this day," said Paul, referring to**   [1 Corinthians 4:9–13]
  - a   the Jews
  - b   the brethren in Christ
  - c   the apostles
  - d   himself and Sosthenes

1258. **Paul was disturbed by reports of fornication that included a man's having his father's**
      [1 Corinthians 5:1–5]
  - a   sister
  - b   brother
  - c   daughter
  - d   wife

1259. **Litigation among the brethren, said Paul, should be settled**   [1 Corinthians 6:1–6]
  - a   in the ordinary courts of law
  - b   by the Lord, through prayer

    c by some wise man among the brethren
    d by the toss of a coin

1260. **Among those who will not inherit the Kingdom of God,
Paul does not name**   [1 Corinthians 6:9–10]
    a fornicators
    b effeminate [men]
    c abusers of themselves
    d masculine [women]

1261. **He who is joined with an harlot, said Paul,**
                                    [1 Corinthians 6:16]
    a becomes one spirit with her
    b creates a gulf between their spirits
    c is one body with her
    d changes nothing with respect to his or her body
        or spirit

1262. **Paul's advice concerning marriage was evidently**
                                    [1 Corinthians 7:1–2]
    a gratuitous
    b supererogatory
    c a reply
    d an inquiry

1263. **Paul's advice concerning marriage was evidently intended for**   [1 Corinthians 7:1–2; 1:2]
    a the general public
    b only members of the church
    c only Jewish members of the church
    d only leaders of the church

1264. **The power of her own body and the power of his own
body is had, says Paul, by**   [1 Corinthians 7:4]
    a the husband and wife, respectively
    b the wife and husband, respectively
    c the wife, in both cases
    d the husband, in both cases

1265. **Paul expressed the wish "that all men were even as I
myself," by which he evidently implied, able to**
                                    [1 Corinthians 7:7–9]
    a remain faithful to one woman
    b give one's wife her conjugal rights
    c abstain from sexual relations
    d avoid gluttony

1266. **"For it is better to marry," said Paul, "than to**
                                    [1 Corinthians 7:8–9]
    a freeze"
    b yearn"
    c burn"
    d hunt"

1267. **An unbelieving husband or wife of a believing spouse should be**   [1 Corinthians 7:12–16]
    a   divorced
    b   divorced or not, as the believing spouse wishes
    c   divorced or not, as the unbelieving spouse wishes
    d   allowed to separate or not, as the unbelieving spouse wishes

1268. **The chief difficulty with marriage, as Paul viewed it, was that it made the married man unduly**
                                        [1 Corinthians 7:32–34]
    a   concerned with his wife's spiritual welfare
    b   concerned with his wife's material welfare
    c   unconcerned with his wife's spiritual welfare
    d   unconcerned with his wife's material welfare

1269. **"I am made all things to all men," said Paul, indicating thereby self-**   [1 Corinthians 9:19–23]
    a   denigration
    b   castigation
    c   approbation
    d   exaltation

1270. **If you accept an unbeliever's invitation to a feast, said Paul,**   [1 Corinthians 10:27]
    a   eat whatever is set before you
    b   eat only what the Hebraic law allows
    c   attend the dinner, but eat nothing
    d   admit your mistake, and revoke your acceptance

1271. **Any man who prays or prophesies, said Paul, should**
                                        [1 Corinthians 11:4]
    a   cover his head
    b   remove his shoes
    c   uncover his head
    d   bare his arms

1272. **Any woman who prays or prophesies, said Paul, should**
                                        [1 Corinthians 11:5]
    a   cover her head
    b   remove her shoes
    c   uncover her head
    d   bare her arms

1273. **That it is a shame to him for a man to wear long hair is, said Paul,**   [1 Corinthians 11:14]
    a   only a popular superstition
    b   attested to by the prophets
    c   applicable only to the disciples
    d   taught by nature itself

1274. **The apparent ranking in importance that Paul implies for the following four (among others) is**
                                        [1 Corinthians 12:28]
    a   prophets, apostles, teachers, healers

b   apostles, prophets, healers, teachers
c   apostles, teachers, prophets, healers
d   apostles, prophets, teachers, healers

1275. **"Though I speak with the tongues of men and of angels,"
said Paul, "I am become as sounding brass, or a
tinkling cymbal,"** if I have not   [1 Corinthians 13:1]
a   faith
b   hope
c   gratitude
d   charity

1276. **"When I was a child,"** I   [1 Corinthians 13:11]
a   spoke, thought, and acted as a child
b   spoke, understood, and thought as a child
c   thought, understood, and acted as a child
d   spoke, understood, and acted as a child

1277. **Compared with one who prophesies, one who speaks
with tongues is**   [1 Corinthians 14:5]
a   less
b   greater
c   the same
d   less, unless he interprets

1278. **Women, in churches, wrote Paul, should**
   [1 Corinthians 14:34]
a   prophesy
b   participate in responses
c   speak in tongues
d   keep silence

1279. **Paul**   [1 Corinthians 15:8]
a   never saw Jesus
b   did see Jesus
c   saw Jesus in a dream
d   may or may not have seen Jesus; he does not tell us

1280. **"Let us eat and drink, for to morrow we**
   [1 Corinthians 15:32]
a   fast"
b   work"
c   die"
d   hunt"

1281. **"At the last trump," wrote Paul, "the dead shall be
raised**   [1 Corinthians 15:52]
a   incorruptible"
b   corruptible"
c   some incorruptible, some corruptible"
d   neither corruptible nor incorruptible"

1282. **"O death, where is thy sting? O grave, where is thy
victory?" asks Paul, and replies to the first question that
it is**   [1 Corinthians 15:55–56]
a   annihilation

    b   uncertainty
    c   loss of love
    d   sin

2 Corinthians

1283. **We learn from Paul's second letter to the Corinthians that in Asia he experienced**   [2 Corinthians 1:8]
    a   exultation
    b   apprehension
    c   remorse
    d   despair

1284. **"But if any have caused grief," wrote Paul,**
                             [2 Corinthians 2:5–7]
    a   rebuke him
    b   ignore him
    c   forgive and comfort him
    d   react according to the circumstances

1285. **To this day, when Moses is read by Israelites, wrote Paul, a veil is**   [2 Corinthians 3:15]
    a   removed from their heart
    b   upon their heart
    c   made translucent
    d   thickened

1286. **We must all appear, according to Paul, in 2 Corinthians 5, before the judgment seat of**   [2 Corinthians 5:10]
    a   God
    b   Christ
    c   the Holy Ghost
    d   the Trinity

1287. **Paul found that the churches in Macedonia gave, to aid the saints,**   [2 Corinthians 8:1–3]
    a   not at all
    b   below their power
    c   only according to their power
    d   beyond their power

1288. **Paul was sending certain brethren to the Corinthians ahead of him so that**   [2 Corinthians 9:3–4]
    a   his own arrival would not be a surprise
    b   they could prepare the Corinthians to receive his message
    c   they could buy off dangerous opponents along that route

    d if he brought some Macedonians with him, he
       would not be ashamed by finding them unprepared

1289. **In his letters, compared to his presence face to face,
Paul was evidently**   [2 Corinthians 10:1, 10]
    a bolder, weightier, and more powerful
    b more humble
    c of the same degree of boldness
    d sometimes bolder, sometimes humbler

1290. **As a speaker Paul evidently thought himself to be**
                     [2 Corinthians 10:10; 11:6]
    a superlative
    b effective
    c average
    d weak

1291. **Paul makes a good deal of the fact that when he was
with the Corinthians he**   [2 Corinthians 11:7–11]
    a accepted generous material support from them
    b received from them only a modest level of material
       support
    c burdened them not at all
    d brought them supplies from Macedonia

1292. **"Are they ministers of Christ? I am more," wrote Paul,
interpolating, "I speak as a**   [2 Corinthians 11:23]
    a saint"
    b sinner"
    c seer"
    d fool"

1293. **Five times, wrote Paul, he had received**
                     [2 Corinthians 11:24]
    a ten stripes save one
    b twenty stripes save one
    c thirty stripes save one
    d forty stripes save one

1294. **"There was given to me a thorn in the flesh," wrote
Paul, to**   [2 Corinthians 12:7-9]
    a create sympathy for me
    b keep me from being too exalted by the abundance
       of the revelations
    c afford occasions for demonstrating how faith can
       heal
    d remind me that the spirit triumphs over the body

Galatians

1295. **The astonishment expressed by Paul in his letter to the Galatians referred to** [Galatians 1:6]
   a   his own achievements
   b   their conduct
   c   the Corinthians' conduct
   d   the state of the world

1296. **The gospel preached by me, wrote Paul, I received from** [Galatians 1:11–12]
   a   another man
   b   two other men
   c   three other men
   d   no man

1297. **While Paul had been entrusted with the gospel to the uncircumcised, the gospel to the circumcised had been entrusted to** [Galatians 2:7–8]
   a   Andrew
   b   James
   c   John
   d   Peter

1298. **Paul opposed Peter to his face, at Antioch, because Peter** [Galatians 2:11–12]
   a   ate with the Gentiles
   b   did not eat with the Gentiles
   c   opposed the circumcision party
   d   sided with the Galatians

1299. **In the fruit of the Spirit Paul did not specifically list** [Galatians 5:22–23]
   a   humbleness
   b   joy
   c   meekness
   d   longsuffering

1300. **"Brethren, if a man be overtaken in a fault, ye which are spiritual, restore such an one in the spirit of** [Galatians 6:1]
   a   meekness"
   b   impartiality"
   c   reproof"
   d   sternness"

1301. **" . . . for whatsoever a man soweth,** [Galatians 6:7]
   a   that shall others also reap"

b   that shall he also reap"
c   that shall he also sow again"
d   readiness is all"

Ephesians

1302. **The "prince of the power of the air" is**
                                          [Ephesians 2:2]
a   beneficent
b   indifferent
c   malign
d   capricious

1303. **You have been saved, wrote Paul,**   [Ephesians 2:8-9]
a   quite through your own efforts
b   not at all through your own efforts
c   partly through your own efforts
d   by my efforts

1304. **To the Gentiles Paul said that Christ had "broken down
the middle wall of partition between us; Having abol-
ished in his flesh**   [Ephesians 2:14-15]
a   the attitude of special dispensation"
b   hatred of any living thing"
c   the enmity, even the law of commandments con-
     tained in ordinances"
d   the spirit of aggression"

1305. **The fact that the Gentiles are "fellowheirs" was, to
earlier generations,**   [Ephesians 3:4-6]
a   not known
b   known, but ignored
c   known, but misinterpreted
d   known, and admitted

1306. **"Let not the sun go down," wrote Paul, "upon your**
                                          [Ephesians 4:26]
a   idleness"
b   wrath"
c   idolatry"
d   faith"

1307. **Paul did not urge that among the brethren there be no**
                                          [Ephesians 5:4, 18-19]
a   foolish talking
b   jesting
c   drunkenness
d   singing

1308. **"Wives, submit yourselves unto your own husbands,"
wrote Paul, and added,** [Ephesians 5:22-25, 33]
    a no widow should remarry
    b except in the raising of children
    c in return for exclusive possession of your husband
    d let each husband love his wife as himself

1309. **It is written, Paul noted, that a man shall "leave his
father and mother, and shall be joined unto his wife,
and they two shall be one flesh," adding that this is**
[Ephesians 5:31-32]
    a self-evident
    b understandable
    c somewhat ambiguous
    d a great mystery

1310. **" 'Honour thy father and mother,' " quoted Paul, noting
that this "is the first commandment with promise;" in
fact,** [Ephesians 6:1-3; Exodus 20:2-17)
    a it is also the last such
    b the promise sets other conditions
    c the promise refers only to life after death
    d it is a promise few would value

1311. **Paul urged servants to** [Ephesians 6:5-8]
    a rebel against their masters
    b be obedient to their masters
    c practice passive nonobedience
    d save, to purchase their freedom

Philippians

1312. **Since "for me to live is Christ, and to die is gain," Paul
wrote that, although having a desire to depart, he knew
he would abide in the flesh, since that was**
[Philippians 1:21-26]
    a the human desire to which he had to remain subject
    b more necessary on the brethren's account
    c something over which he had no choice
    d more necessary on the Gentiles' account

1313. **Timotheus, compared with others of the brethren, was
evidently considered by Paul to be**
[Philippians 2:19-22]

    a somewhat lacking

    b   indistinguishable from them
    c   not easy to rank
    d   clearly superior

1314. **Paul himself was circumcised**   [Philippians 3:5]
    a   not at all
    b   on the eighth day
    c   on his first birthday
    d   when he was an adult

1315. **"And the peace of God, which passeth all understanding, shall**   [Philippians 4:7; 2:2, 15; 3:21]
    a   keep your hearts and minds through Christ Jesus"
    b   change our vile body, that it may be fashioned like unto his glorious body"
    c   make us likeminded, having the same love, being of one accord"
    d   make you without rebuke, in the midst of a crooked and perverse nation"

Colossians

1316. **The letter to the Colossians was sent from Paul and the one who joined him in the**   [Colossians 1:1; 2 Corinthians 1:1]
    a   letter to the Romans
    b   first letter to the Corinthians
    c   second letter to the Corinthians
    d   letter to the Ephesians

1317. **The "handwriting of ordinances that was against us," Jesus**   [Colossians 2:14]
    a   enforced
    b   reinforced
    c   altered
    d   nailed to His cross

1318. **"In meat, or in drink, or in respect of an holy day, or of the new moon, or of the sabbath days," wrote Paul,**   [Colossians 2:16]
    a   obey the authorities
    b   watch others closely
    c   let no man judge you
    d   reach agreement within the group

1319. **The worship of angels was something that Paul**
[Colossians 2:18–19]

    a approved of
    b disapproved of
    c thought worthy of study
    d expressed no opinion on

1320. **"Let your speech be alway with grace," wrote Paul to the Colossians, "seasoned with**   [Colossians 4:6]

    a spice"
    b sweetness"
    c wisdom"
    d salt"

1 Thessalonians

1321. **Paul's opening paragraphs of his first letter to the Thessalonians are, in tone,**   [1 Thessalonians 1:2–10]

    a admonitory
    b declaratory
    c congratulatory
    d sad

1322. **Evidently, the Thessalonians had been visited before, by**
[1 Thessalonians 3:1–6]

    a Paul and Timotheus, at the same time
    b Paul and Timotheus, at different times
    c Paul, but not Timotheus
    d Timotheus, but not Paul

2 Thessalonians

1323. **The Thessalonians are warned to pay no heed to announcements that the day of Christ is at hand, until**
[2 Thessalonians 2:1–4]

    a the stars fall from the heavens and the sun stands still
    b the son of perdition is revealed
    c for a twelve-month period no woman conceives
    d rivers run red

1324. **The tone of Paul's closing paragraphs of his second letter to the Thessalonians is** [2 Thessalonians 3:7–18]
   a   admonitory
   b   declaratory
   c   congratulatory
   d   sad

1325. **If any one refuses to work, wrote Paul, he should**
                         [2 Thessalonians 3:10]
   a   not eat
   b   nevertheless eat
   c   be forced to work
   d   be exiled

1 Timothy

1326. **In his first letter to Timothy, Paul's attitude toward the compilation of long genealogies was one of**
                         [1 Timothy 1:3–4]
   a   enthusiasm
   b   approbation
   c   indifference
   d   scorn

1327. **The reasons given by Paul for permitting no woman to teach or to have authority over men but instead adjuring them to "be in silence" did not include the following:** [1 Timothy 2:12–14]
   a   Adam was formed first
   b   Eve, not Adam, was deceived
   c   Eve became a transgressor
   d   Eve was formed to help Adam

1328. **Woman will be saved, Paul continued (if she continues in faith and charity and holiness, with sobriety) through**
                         [1 Timothy 2:15]
   a   helping man
   b   bearing children
   c   ministering to the sick
   d   participating passively in religious ceremonies

1329. **The list of attributes that Paul set for a bishop did not include the following** [1 Timothy 3:2–3]
   a   blameless
   b   sober
   c   sympathetic
   d   hospitable

1330. **A bishop, wrote Paul, must keep "in subjection with all gravity" his**   [1 Timothy 3:4–5]
    a   children
    b   wife
    c   deacon
    d   congregation

1331. **The list of negatives that Paul specifically set for a deacon happened not to include the following:**
                                 [1 Timothy 3:8–10]
    a   not double-tongued
    b   not given to much wine
    c   not greedy of filthy lucre
    d   not a brawler

1332. **Paul declared that "the Spirit speaketh expressly, that in the latter times some shall depart from the faith, giving heed to seducing spirits, and doctrines of devils; Speaking lies in hypocrisy; having their conscience seared with a hot iron; Forbidding to**
                                 [1 Timothy 4:1–3]
    a   dance"
    b   lend"
    c   marry"
    d   proselyte" ·

1333. **Dietary laws were evidently, in Paul's view,**
                                 [1 Timothy 4:3–5]
    a   necessary
    b   acceptable
    c   rejectable
    d   harmful

1334. **Paul implied that a younger member of the brethren should, with respect to an older man whom he sees in wrongdoing,**   [1 Timothy 5:1]
    a   rebuke
    b   entreat
    c   counsel
    d   remain silent

1335. **"But if any provide not for his own, and specially for those of his own house," wrote Paul, he "is worse than**
                               [1 Timothy 5:8]
    a   a thief"
    b   an usurer"
    c   an embezzler"
    d   an infidel"

1336. **Paul's prescription for younger widows was to**
                            [1 Timothy 5:11–15]
    a   never remarry
    b   remarry but have no children

    c   remarry and have children
    d   make up their own minds

1337. **Paul recommended that those who sinned be rebuked**
                                         [1 Timothy 5:20]
    a   privately
    b   before a judge
    c   before their families
    d   before all

1338. **As to wine, counseled Paul, drink it**   [1 Timothy 5:23]
    a   not at all
    b   only on religious occasions
    c   a little, for thy stomach's sake and thine often infirmities
    d   freely, for thy spirit's sake

1339. **Servants who have believing masters, implied Paul,**
                                         [1 Timothy 6:2]
    a   are relieved of obligation toward them
    b   may serve them somewhat less strenuously than otherwise
    c   should act just as servants of unbelievers
    d   serve them the better because of that

1340. **"The love of money," wrote Paul, "is the**
                                        [1 Timothy 6:10]
    a   spur to ambition"
    b   cement of the family"
    c   source of all controversy"
    d   root of all evil"

2 Timothy

1341. **Lois, referred to in Paul's second letter to Timothy, was Timothy's**   [2 Timothy 1:5]
    a   wife
    b   sister
    c   mother
    d   grandmother

1342. **Eunice was**   [2 Timothy 1:5]
    a   Timothy's sister
    b   Paul's sister
    c   Timothy's mother
    d   Paul's grandmother

1343. **In his closing chapter in 2 Timothy, Paul did not write**
[2 Timothy 4:7]

    a "I have fought a good fight"
    b "I have finished my course"
    c "I have ended the debate"
    d "I have kept the faith"

1344. **"I was delivered out of the mouth of the lion," wrote Paul, referring to his**   [2 Timothy 4:16–17]
    a first defense
    b last trip
    c last illness
    d last temptation

Titus

1345. **Quoting a prophet of Crete to the effect that "Cretians are always liars, evil beasts, slow bellies," in his letter to Titus in Crete, Paul remarked that this is**
[Titus 1:12–13]

    a true
    b false
    c only partly true
    d only partly false

1346. **"Unto the pure," wrote Paul, "all things are**
[Titus 1:15]

    a holy"
    b worthy"
    c harmless"
    d pure"

1347. **Bid the aged women, wrote Paul to Titus, among other things, not to be**   [Titus 2:3]
    a "gossips"
    b "busybodies"
    c "seekers of alms"
    d "given to much wine"

Philemon

1348. **Of the four letters addressed by Paul to particular persons, that to Philemon is the**   [Philemon]
    a longest

b   shortest
c   next to the longest
d   next to the shortest

1349.   **The tone of Paul's letter to Philemon is**   [Philemon]
a   stern
b   gracious
c   questioning
d   pessimistic

Hebrews

1350.   **According to Hebrews, the Son is able to succor those
who are tempted, because He**   [Hebrews 2:18; 1:2]
a   disposes of greater power than the devil
b   is the Son of God
c   Himself has been tempted
d   Himself has been innocent of temptation

1351.   **Every high priest "can have compassion on the ignorant,
and on them that are out of the way;" since he himself
is**   [Hebrews 5:1-2]
a   "knowledgeable and righteous"
b   "compassed with infirmity"
c   "protected by his office"
d   "thoughtful on their spiritual goal"

1352.   **As to those "who were once enlightened" and "were
made partakers of the Holy Ghost," if they fall away,
said Hebrews, they**   [Hebrews 6:4-6]
a   can be renewed to repentance
b   cannot be renewed to repentance
c   can be forgiven
d   can again become apostles

1353.   **When God made a promise to Abraham, He swore by
Himself because**   [Hebrews 6:13]
a   He had no one greater to swear by
b   Abraham asked Him to do so
c   the swearing was a formality in any event
d   "by God!" is not sacrilegious when uttered by God

1354.   **The Lord Jesus was descended from a tribe that had
until then supplied**   [Hebrews 7:13-14]
a   no priests
b   a line of priests alternative to the Levites
c   only an occasional priest
d   one renegade priest

1355. **Jesus was made "a surety of a better testament" because**   [Hebrews 7:20–22]
    a former priests had to take their office with an oath; Jesus did not
    b former priests took their office without an oath; God swore the oath of Jesus' office
    c former priests swore an oath of office themselves; God swore the oath of Jesus' office
    d neither former priests nor Jesus took office with an oath

1356. **Hebrews teaches that the first covenant (with Moses and his people) was**   [Hebrews 8:7–13]
    a faultless
    b faulty
    c obscure
    d legally vulnerable

1357. **The Holiest of all, Hebrews recalls, was the**
                    [Hebrews 9:3–4]
    a manna in the golden pot in the ark of the covenant in the tabernacle behind the second vail
    b golden pot in the ark of the covenant in the tabernacle behind the second vail
    c ark of the covenant in the tabernacle behind the second vail
    d tabernacle behind the second vail

1358. **When Christ appears a second time, says Hebrews, it will be to**   [Hebrews 9:28]
    a deal with sin
    b confirm the prophecies
    c save those who look for Him
    d save everyone

1359. **"It is a fearful thing to fall into the hands of**
                    [Hebrews 10:31]
    a Satan"
    b the secular authorities"
    c the living God"
    d the apostles"

1360. **As an example of faith, Hebrews recalls the actions of**
                    [Hebrews 11:4]
    a Adam
    b Eve
    c Cain
    d Abel

1361. **Our correction by God differs from our correction by our earthly fathers, in that His correction is**
                    [Hebrews 12:9–10]
    a far more severe

b   for our own good
c   arbitrary
d   only for a short time

1362.   **Esau is given, in Hebrews, as an example of one who**
                                            [Hebrews 12:16–17]
a   spurned an opportunity to repent
b   never attempted to repent
c   was given no chance to repent
d   repented and was saved

1363.   **"Be not forgetful to entertain strangers," says Hebrews,
        "for thereby**   [Hebrews 13:2]
a   others will show hospitality unto you"
b   the living God will be pleased"
c   some have entertained angels unawares"
d   we acknowledge that we are all strangers but in
        God"

James

1364.   **James, in his letter to the twelve tribes scattered
        abroad, emphasized the need, in asking God for wisdom,
        to do so in faith, with**   [James 1:1, 5–8]
a   humility
b   determination to act
c   no wavering
d   others of the brethren

1365.   **Anyone who is a hearer of the word and not a doer,
        said James, is like a man who beholds** [James 1:23–24]
a   the passing crowd in the street
b   the moon and stars in the sky
c   the unopened books on the shelves
d   his face in a glass

1366.   **Faith, wrote James,**   [James 2:17–26]
a   is enough to save a man, without works
b   is not needed, if there are works
c   if it has no works, is dead
d   even with works is not necessarily enough

1367.   **The opinion that James held of the human tongue
        seems on the whole to have been** [James 3:5–12]
a   extravagantly favorable
b   cautiously favorable
c   somewhat unfavorable
d   decidedly unfavorable

1368. **"Let your yea be yea, and your nay, nay," urged James, instead of** [James 5:12]
   a   qualifying every assertion
   b   indulging in indecisiveness
   c   swearing
   d   sulking

1 Peter

1369. **In his first letter, Peter adjured "strangers scattered throughout" several lands:** [1 Peter 1:1; 2:17]
   a   Love the brotherhood. Honour God. Fear the king
   b   Honour the brotherhood. Love God. Fear the king
   c   Fear the brotherhood. Love God. Honour the king
   d   Love the brotherhood. Fear God. Honour the king

1370. **To servants, Peter implied that it was not to their credit if, when they did wrong and were buffeted for it, they took it patiently, since** [1 Peter 2:20]
   a   an abject bearing towards a fellow man was not acceptable to God
   b   any wrongdoer might expect to suffer accordingly
   c   servants are fortunate to escape with a buffeting
   d   all servants have their turn, eventually

1371. **Submissiveness in wives of the brethren would, by Peter's reasoning, yield beneficial results through a comparison of those wives with wives of nonbelievers, made by** [1 Peter 3:1–2]
   a   brethren husbands
   b   nonbelieving husbands
   c   wives of nonbelievers
   d   brethren wives

1372. **Peter characterized** [1 Peter 3:7]
   a   woman as the weaker
   b   man as the stronger
   c   woman as the stronger
   d   man and woman as equal in essential strength

1373. **Do not, wrote Peter, return** [1 Peter 3:9]
   a   evil for good
   b   evil for evil

  c good for evil
  d good for good

1374. **It is better to suffer, wrote Peter, if that should be God's will, for**   [1 Peter 3:17]
  a wel! doing than for evil doing
  b evil doing than for well doing
  c evil doing than for right thinking
  d right thinking than for evil doing

1375. **The "multitude of sins" is covered, wrote Peter, by**
                  [1 Peter 4:8]
  a faith
  b charity
  c hate
  d meekness

1376. **"Your adversary the devil," warned Peter,** [1 Peter 5:8]
  a glides about as a deceiving serpent
  b walks about as a roaring lion
  c steps around as a silent cat
  d hovers around as a devouring vulture

2 Peter

1377. **In his second letter, Peter explains that the prophecies of Scripture are a matter of private interpretation**
                [2 Peter 1:20]
  a never
  b always
  c rarely
  d often

1378. **"The dog is turned to his own vomit again," said Peter, referring to the**   [2 Peter 2:20–22]
  a sinful who resist reform
  b former sinful who relapse
  c hitherto blameless who turn to sin
  d emperor

1379. **Next time, Peter intimated, the world will be destroyed not by**   [2 Peter 3:5–7]
  a water but by fire
  b water but by ice
  c fire but by ice
  d ice but by fire

1380. **"With the Lord," wrote Peter,**   [2 Peter 3:8]
    a one day is as a thousand years
    b a thousand years are as one day
    c one day is as a thousand years, and a thousand years as one day
    d one day is as the last syllable of recorded time

1 John

1381. **In his first letter, John said that if we say we have fellowship with God while we walk in darkness, we**
                                        [1 John 1:6]
    a lie
    b presume
    c equivocate
    d concede

1382. **"The truth is not in us," wrote John, "if we say that we**
                                          [1 John 1:8]
    a have never sinned"
    b have no sin"
    c shall have no sin"
    d know not sin"

1383. **"Whosoever hateth his brother," wrote John, "is a**
                                         [1 John 3:15]
    a thief"
    b cheat"
    c embezzler"
    d murderer"

1384. **"God," wrote John, "is**   [1 John 4:8]
    a majesty"
    b omnipotence'"
    c love"
    d forgiveness"

2 John

1385. **In his second letter, John wrote that "If there come any unto you, and bring not this doctrine [of Christ],**
                                         [2 John 1:10]
    a receive him into your house and seek to make him believe"

b   receive him into your house but argue not with
    him"
c   receive him not into your house"
d   leave the house yourself"

3 John

1386. **In his third letter, John refers to the Gentiles in the
       context of**   [3 John 1:5-7]
       a   his attempts to convert them
       b   their sure loss of eternal life
       c   nonacceptance by the brethren of aid from them
       d   a distinction between types of Gentiles

Jude

1387. **The letter of Jude expressed concern over impairment
       of the morale of the brethren arising from**   [Jude 1:4]
       a   avariciousness
       b   lasciviousness
       c   ambitiousness
       d   unnutritiousness

1388. **Jude pointed out that when the Archangel Michael,
       contending with the devil, disputed about the body of
       Moses, he**   [Jude 1:9]
       a   rebuked the devil
       b   did not rebuke the devil
       c   acknowledged that he understood the devil's point
           of view but did not accept it
       d   came close to being persuaded by the devil

The Revelation

1389. **The Revelation of Jesus Christ was given to Him by
       God, and then transmitted by His angel to John to show
       His servants what must take place**   [Revelation 1:1, 3]

   a shortly
   b in the not too distant future
   c eventually
   d after what will seem to men an interminable period
      of suffering

1390. **"I am Alpha and Omega," said**   [Revelation 1:8]
   a Jesus
   b the Lord, the Almighty
   c Satan
   d Michael

1391. **The seven churches to which John was to send his account of the revelation included**   [Revelation 1:11, 4]
   a Alexandria
   b Benecia
   c Peoria
   d Philadelphia

1392. **The one who spoke to John stood in the midst of golden candlesticks, and in his right hand held stars, to the number of**   [Revelation 1:12–13, 16]
   a three
   b seven
   c thirteen
   d forty

1393. **Out of the speaker's mouth there went a**
                                   [Revelation 1:16]
   a tongue of fire
   b lance of bronze
   c two-edged sword
   d plume of smoke

1394. **The Spirit commanded John to send the angel of the church in Ephesus a reprimand for inadequacy in**
                                 [Revelation 2:2–4]
   a toil
   b patience
   c love
   d hatred

1395. **With the church in Philadelphia the Spirit was evidently**
                     [Revelation 3:7–13; 2:29]
   a well pleased
   b moderately pleased
   c moderately unhappy
   d quite unhappy

1396. **The Spirit was greatly displeased by the Laodiceans' conduct, it was so**   [Revelation 3:14–16]
   a extravagant
   b cruel
   c blundering
   d lukewarm

1397. **When the door opened in heaven and John was taken up with the Spirit he saw a throne surrounded by seats to the number of** [Revelation 4:1–4]
   a three
   b seven
   c twenty-four
   d forty

1398. **"No man in heaven, nor in earth, neither under the earth" was able to open the book sealed with the seven seals save** [Revelation 5:3–8]
   a the twenty-four elders in white on the surrounding seats
   b the Archangel Michael
   c the Lamb standing, as though it had been slain, with seven horns and with seven eyes
   d the four living beasts

1399. **The four horsemen of the Apocalpyse appeared on horses of the following colors, in the order given:** [Revelation 6:1–8]
   a red, white, black, pale
   b white, pale, red, black
   c black, white, red, pale
   d white, red, black, pale

1400. **The rider of the red horse was permitted to** [Revelation 6:4]
   a kill with sword, and with hunger, and with death, and with the beasts of the earth
   b take peace from the earth so that men should kill one another
   c conquer
   d annihilate with earthquakes

1401. **The rider of the black horse held in his hand a** [Revelation 6:5]
   a sword
   b cross
   c pair of balances
   d rope

1402. **The rider named Death was followed by** [Revelation 6:8]
   a Satan
   b Michael
   c four angels with trumpets
   d Hell

1403. **When the souls of those who had been slain for the Word of God cried out for judgment and vengeance, they were each given a white robe and told** [Revelation 6:9–11]
   a to avenge themselves, with the aid of the horsemen

b   that they should never demand vengeance
c   to wait for more to be killed as they had been
d   to pray

1404.   **When the Lamb "had opened the seventh seal, there was silence in heaven about . . . half**   [Revelation 8:1]
a   a second"
b   a minute"
c   an hour"
d   a year"

1405.   **When the first of the seven angels who stood before God sounded his trumpet, the third part of the**
                            [Revelation 8:7]
a   creatures in the sea died
b   waters became wormwood
c   sun, moon, and stars was smitten
d   trees was burnt up

1406.   **When the star fallen down from heaven to earth was given the key of the bottomless pit and opened it, after the fifth angel had sounded his trumpet, the locusts that emerged were told to**   [Revelation 9:1–5]
a   consume all mankind's stocks of food within seven months
b   strip the earth bare of grass within six months
c   blanket the earth from the sun for seven years
d   torment for five months those of mankind without the seal of God in their foreheads

1407.   **When the sixth angel sounded his trumpet and released the four angels bound in the great river, Euphrates, a third of mankind was killed by**
                            [Revelation 9:13–14, 18]
a   hail, fire, and water
b   fire, smoke, and hail
c   fire, smoke, and brimstone
d   fire, hail, and boils

1408.   **"The beast that ascendeth out of the bottomless pit" was to make war upon**   [Revelation 11:3–8]
a   the remaining two-thirds of mankind
b   the two witnesses who were given power to prophesy for 1,260 days
c   seven thousand people in the city
d   John

1409.   **After the seventh angel had sounded his trumpet there appeared a great red dragon, whose tail**
                            [Revelation 11:15; 12:3–4]
a   swept the third part of the land into the oceans
b   cast the third part of mankind down the open shaft of the bottomless pit

c   forced the third part of the angels down to earth
d   drew the third part of the stars of heaven and cast
them to the earth

1410. **Michael and his angels, fighting in heaven against the
dragon and his angels, defeated them and**
[Revelation 12:7–9]
a   threw them into outer space
b   disintegrated them
c   cast them out into the earth
d   threw them down the bottomless pit

1411. **The composite beast that John saw rising out of the
sea**   [Revelation 13:2, 4]
a   fought the dragon for his power, his seat, and his
great authority
b   shared with the dragon his power, his seat, and
his great authority
c   was given by the dragon his power, his seat, and his
great authority
d   was the dragon in metamorphosis

1412. **The beast was allowed to make war against the saints,**
[Revelation 13:7]
a   but was conquered by them
b   and to overcome them
c   with a stalemate outcome
d   forever

1413. **The mark of the beast, in one's right hand or in one's
forehead (or the name of the beast, or the number of
his name) was necessary in order to**
[Revelation 13:16–17]
a   vote
b   travel
c   buy or sell
d   prophesy

1414. **The number of the beast was**   [Revelation 13:18]
a   13
b   40
c   666
d   777

1415. **On the foreheads of the 144,000 who stood on mount
Sion with the Lamb there was written** [Revelation 14:1]
a   nothing
b   the name of the beast with a stroke through it
c   the name of the Father of the Lamb
d   alpha and omega

1416. **Of the angels that John saw flying in midheaven, the
third announced that any one who worshiped the beast
and his image and received his mark in his forehead or
his hand would be**   [Revelation 14:9–11]

     a mown down with the sickle
     b tormented with fire and brimstone
     c thrown down the shaft of the bottomless pit
     d handed over to the beast

1417. **Armageddon is the place where three unclean spirits like frogs were to assemble the**   [Revelation 16:13–16]
     a kings of the whole world
     b leaders of the twelve tribes
     c unsealed millions
     d the archangels and the demons

1418. **When the seventh angel had poured out his vial into the air and a great voice came from the throne, "It is done," the elements responded with a**
                                       [Revelation 16:17–21]
     a preternatural silence
     b resumption of normal weather
     c violent meteorological display
     d steady rain

1419. **The great whore with whom the kings of the earth had committed fornication was a**   [Revelation 17:1–4]
     a woman sitting on a scarlet beast
     b scarlet woman sitting on a black beast
     c scarlet woman leading a scarlet beast
     d woman sitting on a beast [color unspecified]

1420. **The ten who would receive power as kings for one hour, giving their power and strength unto the beast, were to**
                                       [Revelation 17:12–17]
     a advance the whore's fortunes
     b leave the whore in *status quo*
     c destroy the whore
     d cause to arise a second whore

1421. **The great whore represented**   [Revelation 17:18]
     a a tribe
     b a city
     c a kingdom
     d mankind

1422. **The being with eyes like a flame of fire, clothed with a vesture dipped in blood, who was to tread "the winepress of the fierceness and wrath of Almighty God," sat on a white horse**   [Revelation 19:11–15]
     a called Faithful and True
     b and was called Faithful and True
     c called Faithful, his own name being True
     d called True, his own name being Faithful

1423. **The Devil and Satan was the**   [Revelation 20:2]
     a first beast
     b second beast

    c   dragon
    d   whore

1424. **The Devil and Satan was bound and put away for**
                        [Revelation 20:2]
    a   10 years
    b   100 years
    c   1000 years
    d   forever

1425. **At the first resurrection, there came to life**
                    [Revelation 20:4–6]
    a   all the dead
    b   all the dead who were to be judged, some unfavorably
    c   only the dead who were to be judged favorably
    d   all the dead who were to be returned to death

1426. **In the second battle, the saints**   [Revelation 20:9]
    a   won easily
    b   were saved by fire from heaven
    c   fought to a draw
    d   won when the first beast repented

1427. **Torment forever, day and night, in the lake of fire and brimstone, was the lot of the**   [Revelation 20:10]
    a   devil
    b   devil, the beast, and the false prophet
    c   devil, the beast, the false prophet, and the whore
    d   devil and the whore

1428. **John saw "the dead, small and great, stand before God; and the books were opened," and also "the book of life," and the dead were judged by what was written in the books as to what they had**   [Revelation 20:12]
    a   done
    b   said
    c   believed
    d   seen

1429. **Thrown into the lake of fire were all those whose names were**   [Revelation 20:15]
    a   not in any of the books
    b   in the books more than once
    c   not in the book of life
    d   in the book of death

1430. **John saw the holy city, new Jerusalem,**
                    [Revelation 21:2]
    a   arising out of the sea
    b   coming down out of heaven
    c   springing up suddenly from nowhere
    d   being built by the angels

1431. **In the new Jerusalem there will be no more**
[Revelation 21:4]

    a death, sorrow, crying, pain
    b sorrow, crying, pain
    c crying, pain
    d pain

1432. **He who sat upon the throne declared to John that He was Alpha and Omega, that is, the**
[Revelation 21:5–6]

    a beginning and the end
    b end and the beginning
    c first and second end
    d first and second beginning

1433. **The wall of the city was built of jasper, and the city itself, like unto clear glass, was pure**
[Revelation 21:18]

    a gold
    b diamonds
    c quartz
    d ice

1434. **The new city had**   [Revelation 21:22]
    a no temple
    b one temple
    c twelve temples
    d forty temples

1435. **John was shown the river of water of life, clear as crystal, proceeding**   [Revelation 22:1–2]
    a around the city
    b by the side of the city street
    c out of the throne of God and of the Lamb
    d directly into the fountain in the center of the city

1436. **In the new city they will**   [Revelation 22:4]
    a still not see His face
    b see His face
    c not desire to see His face
    d see only the reflection of His face in the river

1437. **The angel who had shown John these things said at the end,**   [Revelation 22:10]
    a "seal up the sayings of the prophecy of this book"
    b "seal up this book save the words of prophecy"
    c "seal not the sayings of the prophecy of this book"
    d "seal up this book for one thousand years"

Answers

1 a	47 b	93 d	139 c	185 c	231 a	277 b
2 c	48 a	94 b	140 a	186 a	232 c	278 c
3 b	49 b	95 b	141 a	187 c	233 c	279 c
4 c	50 b	96 c	142 b	188 d	234 d	280 a
5 c	51 d	97 a	143 a	189 a	235 a	281 b
6 a	52 d	98 c	144 d	190 a	236 b	282 a
7 a	53 a	99 b	145 b	191 c	237 a	283 d
8 b	54 b	100 c	146 a	192 d	238 c	284 a
9 a	55 b	101 a	147 d	193 a	239 c	285 a
10 a	56 c	102 a	148 a	194 b	240 b	286 c
11 d	57 d	103 b	149 b	195 c	241 b	287 b
12 a	58 b	104 b	150 a	196 d	242 a	288 a
13 a	59 a	105 d	151 b	197 c	243 a	289 c
14 b	60 d	106 a	152 c	198 c	244 c	290 b
15 a	61 b	107 b	153 a	199 c	245 b	291 c
16 b	62 c	108 c	154 a	200 a	246 b	292 b
17 d	63 c	109 d	155 b	201 a	247 d	293 c
18 d	64 d	110 a	156 a	202 b	248 b	294 a
19 a	65 c	111 c	157 d	203 a	249 a	295 c
20 c	66 c	112 c	158 c	204 d	250 a	296 b
21 a	67 a	113 a	159 a	205 a	251 a	297 c
22 d	68 b	114 c	160 b	206 b	252 c	298 a
23 a	69 d	115 d	161 b	207 b	253 c	299 c
24 c	70 b	116 b	162 c	208 c	254 a	300 a
25 c	71 b	117 b	163 c	209 d	255 b	301 b
26 a	72 a	118 b	164 a	210 c	256 b	302 d
27 d	73 a	119 a	165 b	211 b	257 b	303 d
28 b	74 b	120 a	166 d	212 a	258 a	304 a
29 a	75 b	121 a	167 c	213 d	259 d	305 c
30 b	76 c	122 d	168 c	214 c	260 b	306 a
31 a	77 a	123 c	169 c	215 d	261 a	307 c
32 a	78 b	124 a	170 b	216 c	262 d	308 a
33 a	79 d	125 b	171 d	217 a	263 c	309 b
34 c	80 d	126 a	172 d	218 d	264 b	310 b
35 b	81 b	127 b	173 c	219 d	265 b	311 a
36 b	82 a	128 c	174 d	220 c	266 a	312 c
37 b	83 d	129 c	175 c	221 d	267 a	313 a
38 b	84 c	130 b	176 a	222 c	268 c	314 a
39 d	85 a	131 a	177 b	223 a	269 a	315 b
40 a	86 a	132 a	178 a	224 b	270 d	316 a
41 c	87 a	133 a	179 c	225 d	271 a	317 d
42 a	88 c	134 c	180 b	226 d	272 c	318 d
43 a	89 a	135 a	181 d	227 c	273 c	319 b
44 b	90 b	136 d	182 c	228 b	274 d	320 d
45 b	91 d	137 b	183 b	229 d	275 a	321 b
46 b	92 b	138 a	184 c	230 a	276 a	322 c

323 b	375 c	427 b	479 b	531 c	583 a	635 c
324 a	376 a	428 a	480 c	532 c	584 a	636 c
325 d	377 c	429 c	481 a	533 a	585 b	637 c
326 a	378 d	430 b	482 a	534 c	586 c	638 c
327 b	379 d	431 c	483 d	535 a	587 b	639 c
328 d	380 d	432 b	484 b	536 b	588 a	640 c
329 d	381 a	433 d	485 a	537 a	589 b	641 d
330 a	382 a	434 a	486 b	538 a	590 d	642 d
331 b	383 c	435 c	487 b	539 c	591 c	643 b
332 b	384 c	436 b	488 d	540 b	592 b	644 d
333 d	385 d	437 a	489 c	541 b	593 b	645 a
334 c	386 c	438 c	490 d	542 c	594 c	646 d
335 a	387 b	439 c	491 d	543 a	595 d	647 c
336 b	388 d	440 d	492 a	544 d	596 d	648 a
337 c	389 d	441 b	493 d	545 d	597 c	649 d
338 d	390 d	442 a	494 a	546 a	598 b	650 d
339 a	391 c	443 c	495 c	547 d	599 d	651 b
340 a	392 a	444 d	496 c	548 c	600 d	652 c
341 a	393 b	445 c	497 a	549 a	601 c	653 a
342 b	394 c	446 c	498 c	550 a	602 d	654 c
343 b	395 c	447 a	499 c	551 b	603 a	655 c
344 d	396 a	448 a	500 a	552 c	604 d	656 c
345 a	397 a	449 a	501 b	553 b	605 a	657 a
346 a	398 a	450 b	502 c	554 d	606 c	658 d
347 d	399 b	451 b	503 b	555 b	607 a	659 d
348 c	400 b	452 c	504 d	556 b	608 b	660 d
349 d	401 a	453 c	505 a	557 c	609 a	661 a
350 b	402 b	454 b	506 c	558 d	610 b	662 c
351 d	403 a	455 c	507 b	559 d	611 d	663 d
352 d	404 c	456 a	508 a	560 d	612 b	664 b
353 c	405 a	457 d	509 d	561 a	613 d	665 a
354 b	406 a	458 a	510 d	562 b	614 c	666 c
355 d	407 d	459 b	511 a	563 c	615 b	667 c
356 d	408 b	460 d	512 c	564 b	616 c	668 b
357 c	409 a	461 c	513 b	565 c	617 b	669 b
358 b	410 b	462 b	514 d	566 c	618 d	670 d
359 c	411 d	463 b	515 c	567 b	619 b	671 c
360 d	412 c	464 b	516 a	568 d	620 c	672 b
361 d	413 a	465 d	517 d	569 c	621 b	673 a
362 d	414 d	466 c	518 a	570 d	622 b	674 a
363 a	415 d	467 d	519 d	571 c	623 c	675 c
364 a	416 b	468 b	520 d	572 a	624 d	676 c
365 d	417 b	469 a	521 c	573 d	625 a	677 a
366 d	418 d	470 a	522 a	574 c	626 c	678 b
367 d	419 b	471 b	523 d	575 b	627 b	679 c
368 c	420 a	472 b	524 c	576 c	628 d	680 c
369 a	421 d	473 d	525 a	577 a	629 c	681 b
370 c	422 b	474 a	526 b	578 b	630 b	682 c
371 c	423 b	475 b	527 b	579 c	631 c	683 d
372 d	424 b	476 d	528 c	580 c	632 d	684 b
373 d	425 a	477 b	529 a	581 d	633 a	685 c
374 b	426 d	478 d	530 d	582 c	634 b	686 d

687 a	739 a	791 d	843 b	895 d	947 b	999 a
688 c	740 c	792 c	844 c	896 a	948 c	1000 a
689 d	741 a	793 d	845 c	897 b	949 d	1001 b
690 d	742 b	794 a	846 d	898 b	950 b	1002 c
691 b	743 b	795 c	847 d	899 c	951 c	1003 c
692 c	744 a	796 d	848 d	900 b	952 c	1004 c
693 d	745 c	797 b	849 d	901 a	953 c	1005 b
694 b	746 a	798 a	850 a	902 d	954 b	1006 d
695 d	747 b	799 d	851 b	903 b	955 d	1007 a
696 c	748 b	800 c	852 c	904 a	956 a	1008 b
697 d	749 d	801 b	853 d	905 b	957 b	1009 c
698 d	750 d	802 b	854 a	906 a	958 d	1010 b
699 b	751 d	803 b	855 d	907 a	959 c	1011 d
700 d	752 c	804 a	856 a	908 b	960 c	1012 c
701 b	753 b	805 a	857 b	909 a	961 d	1013 c
702 d	754 c	806 b	858 c	910 b	962 a	1014 a
703 a	755 a	807 c	859 c	911 d	963 a	1015 c
704 c	756 b	808 b	860 b	912 c	964 a	1016 d
705 b	757 d	809 c	861 c	913 c	965 b	1017 a
706 c	758 b	810 d	862 d	914 a	966 c	1018 a
707 a	759 a	811 b	863 b	915 a	967 c	1019 d
708 b	760 b	812 c	864 c	916 c	968 a	1020 d
709 a	761 d	813 d	865 c	917 d	969 c	1021 b
710 d	762 a	814 b	866 d	918 c	970 c	1022 c
711 b	763 b	815 d	867 c	919 c	971 d	1023 c
712 d	764 a	816 b	868 b	920 d	972 a	1024 c
713 b	765 b	817 a	869 a	921 b	973 b	1025 a
714 d	766 c	818 c	870 a	922 a	974 c	1026 b
715 d	767 c	819 c	871 c	923 c	975 a	1027 c
716 c	768 b	820 c	872 d	924 c	976 b	1028 c
717 c	769 b	821 d	873 b	925 a	977 c	1029 d
718 d	770 a	822 a	874 a	926 b	978 d	1030 c
719 a	771 c	823 b	875 c	927 c	979 c	1031 b
720 b	772 c	824 d	876 a	928 d	980 c	1032 c
721 b	773 b	825 d	877 b	929 a	981 b	1033 c
722 c	774 d	826 b	878 b	930 d	982 a	1034 d
723 c	775 a	827 a	879 d	931 b	983 d	1035 b
724 d	776 a	828 a	880 d	932 c	984 b	1036 c
725 a	777 b	829 a	881 a	933 d	985 c	1037 c
726 c	778 c	830 b	882 a	934 a	986 d	1038 a
727 b	779 a	831 a	883 d	935 a	987 d	1039 b
728 d	780 d	832 d	884 d	936 b	988 d	1040 c
729 b	781 b	833 d	885 b	937 c	989 a	1041 a
730 b	782 b	834 b	886 b	938 a	990 b	1042 b
731 c	783 b	835 a	887 a	939 c	991 a	1043 b
732 b	784 b	836 b	888 b	940 d	992 b	1044 d
733 d	785 c	837 c	889 d	941 b	993 c	1045 b
734 d	786 b	838 b	890 c	942 b	994 b	1046 c
735 b	787 c	839 b	891 d	943 a	995 d	1047 b
736 c	788 a	840 b	892 c	944 d	996 a	1048 b
737 c	789 c	841 c	893 c	945 b	997 d	1049 a
738 a	790 b	842 d	894 a	946 c	998 c	1050 d

1051 b	1103 a	1155 b	1207 c	1259 c	1311 b	1363 c
1052 b	1104 b	1156 d	1208 c	1260 d	1312 b	1364 c
1053 b	1105 c	1157 b	1209 a	1261 c	1313 d	1365 c
1054 d	1106 c	1158 d	1210 b	1262 c	1314 b	1366 c
1055 a	1107 b	1159 c	1211 b	1263 b	1315 a	1367 d
1056 c	1108 d	1160 a	1212 c	1264 a	1316 c	1368 c
1057 c	1109 b	1161 b	1213 d	1265 c	1317 d	1369 d
1058 a	1110 a	1162 a	1214 b	1266 a	1318 c	1370 b
1059 c	1111 d	1163 d	1215 a	1267 d	1319 b	1371 b
1060 c	1112 d	1164 b	1216 d	1268 b	1320 d	1372 a
1061 b	1113 d	1165 b	1217 a	1269 c	1321 c	1373 b
1062 c	1114 d	1166 c	1218 b	1270 a	1322 b	1374 a
1063 a	1115 b	1167 c	1219 c	1271 c	1323 b	1375 b
1064 b	1116 c	1168 d	1220 b	1272 a	1324 a	1376 b
1065 c	1117 c	1169 b	1221 a	1273 d	1325 a	1377 a
1066 c	1118 c	1170 c	1222 b	1274 d	1326 d	1378 b
1067 b	1119 c	1171 b	1223 b	1275 d	1327 d	1379 a
1068 c	1120 b	1172 d	1224 c	1276 b	1328 b	1380 c
1069 a	1121 d	1173 c	1225 d	1277 d	1329 c	1381 a
1070 c	1122 c	1174 a	1226 b	1278 d	1330 a	1382 b
1071 c	1123 b	1175 c	1227 c	1279 b	1331 d	1383 d
1072 c	1124 d	1176 d	1228 c	1280 c	1332 c	1384 c
1073 d	1125 b	1177 b	1229 d	1281 a	1333 d	1385 c
1074 d	1126 b	1178 c	1230 d	1282 d	1334 b	1386 c
1075 b	1127 c	1179 d	1231 c	1283 d	1335 d	1387 b
1076 c	1128 c	1180 c	1232 a	1284 c	1336 c	1388 b
1077 b	1129 a	1181 a	1233 d	1285 b	1337 d	1389 a
1078 b	1130 d	1182 b	1234 a	1286 b	1338 c	1390 b
1079 c	1131 b	1183 a	1235 c	1287 d	1339 d	1391 d
1080 a	1132 a	1184 a	1236 a	1288 d	1340 d	1392 b
1081 c	1133 b	1185 d	1237 d	1289 a	1341 d	1393 c
1082 d	1134 c	1186 c	1238 b	1290 d	1342 c	1394 c
1083 c	1135 c	1187 b	1239 a	1291 c	1343 c	1395 a
1084 a	1136 c	1188 d	1240 c	1292 d	1344 a	1396 c
1085 b	1137 b	1189 b	1241 c	1293 d	1345 a	1397 c
1086 d	1138 c	1190 a	1242 c	1294 b	1346 d	1398 c
1087 a	1139 b	1191 c	1243 b	1295 b	1347 d	1399 d
1088 c	1140 d	1192 d	1244 a	1296 d	1348 b	1400 b
1089 c	1141 c	1193 c	1245 d	1297 d	1349 b	1401 c
1090 a	1142 b	1194 a	1246 b	1298 b	1350 c	1402 d
1091 c	1143 b	1195 c	1247 c	1299 a	1351 b	1403 c
1092 c	1144 a	1196 c	1248 b	1300 a	1352 b	1404 c
1093 b	1145 c	1197 b	1249 a	1301 b	1353 a	1405 d
1094 a	1146 d	1198 d	1250 b	1302 c	1354 a	1406 d
1095 b	1147 d	1199 c	1251 d	1303 b	1355 b	1407 c
1096 a	1148 b	1200 c	1252 c	1304 c	1356 b	1408 b
1097 b	1149 c	1201 c	1253 b	1305 a	1357 d	1409 d
1098 d	1150 c	1202 a	1254 a	1306 b	1358 c	1410 c
1099 a	1151 c	1203 b	1255 b	1307 d	1359 c	1411 c
1100 c	1152 d	1204 d	1256 d	1308 d	1360 d	1412 b
1101 b	1153 c	1205 b	1257 c	1309 d	1361 b	1413 c
1102 a	1154 a	1206 a	1258 d	1310 a	1362 c	1414 c

1415 c	1419 a	1423 c	1426 b	1429 c	1432 a	1435 c
1416 b	1420 c	1424 c	1427 b	1430 b	1433 a	1436 b
1417 a	1421 b	1425 c	1428 a	1431 a	1434 a	1437 c
1418 c	1422 b